Fun and Strategies
for TOEIC®
Listening & Reading Test

Yukihiro Tsukada

EIHŌSHA

音声ファイルのダウンロード方法

英宝社ホームページ（http://www.eihosha.co.jp/）の
「テキスト音声ダウンロード」バナーをクリックすると、
音声ファイルダウンロードページにアクセスできます。

はじめに

■ TOEIC テストを知ろう！

　TOEIC テストは、今や年間 200 万人以上が受験する検定試験です。大学生や社会人に求められる英語力測定テストでは最大級。ですが、読者の皆さんは、ただやみくもに受験しているだけ、になっていませんか？

　本書は、TOEIC テストの初級者から中級者を意識し、スコアアップに主眼を置いたテキストです。本番そっくりな問題、即効性のあるテクニック、頻出の単語やフレーズを収録し、TOEIC テストの重要項目を詰め込みました。本書を通じて、どうすればスコアがアップするのか、どのように実用英語やビジネス英語に応用できるのかを学びましょう。

■情報処理のスピードを上げよう！

　TOEIC テストは、L＆R（リスニング＆リーディング）に限定しても、2 時間で 200 問を解くハードなテストです。一般的な「英語力」をじわじわと上げれば、TOEIC テストのスコアもじわじわ上がる、というのは幻想に過ぎません。TOEIC テストでは、大量の問題を短時間に処理する能力が求められるのです。

　重要なのは、「効率」と「処理スピード」。どこにポイントがあり、どうすれば解けるのか。この点をつねに意識しましょう。短時間で最大の効果を上げられるように、ムダを省いた学習をする必要があります。

■テクニックとパターン、そして反復！

　TOEIC テストは、資格試験である以上、一定のテクニックが有効です。ですが、それにはテストパターンを把握し、ナチュラルに反応できるほど反復学習することも大事なのです。

　本書の各章では、本番さながらのスタイルを取っています。つまり、「オフィス」や「交通」などのテーマで、各章を分けていません。本番スタイルのなかで、実践的なテクニックとパターンを学んで下さい。何度も繰り返すことで、それらを完璧に身につけましょう。

　TOEIC テストは、一般的な英語力向上へのゲートウェイです。TOEIC テストの文書パターンは、ビジネス会話や文書に応用できるだけでなく、総合的な英語力の血肉となります。まずは、本書から始めましょう。

　　　　　　　　　　　　　　　　　　　　　　　　　　　塚田　幸光

CONTENTS

TOEIC テストでは、出題パターンを攻略することが大事です。まずは、Part1 から Part7 の基本的な問題と解き方（TIPS）に触れて、TOEIC テストのパターンを確認しましょう。頻出語句のチェックも忘れずに！

part 1   2

Look at the picture and choose the statement that best describes what you see.

1. (A) (B) (C) (D)

2. (A) (B) (C) (D)

☑ **TIPS-1**

「動作」をキャッチしよう！
⇒人物写真では、動作（動詞）を聞き取るのが基本！

☐ put on　～をかぶる
☐ plastic bag
　 ビニール袋
☐ polish　～を拭く
☐ place A on B
　 A を B に置く

☑ **TIPS-2**

写真にないものは×！
⇒写真に写っていないワードを選んではダメ

☐ in either direction
　 両方向に
☐ lean against ～
　 ～に寄りかかる
☐ be reflected
　 反射される

Choose the best response to each question or statement.

3. (A) (B) (C)

4. (A) (B) (C)

5. (A) (B) (C)

Listen to a short conversation, and choose the best answer to each question.

6. Where are the speakers?
(A) In a flower shop
(B) In a restaurant
(C) In a hotel
(D) In an appliance store

7. What does the man give advice about?
(A) Choosing suppliers
(B) Ordering stock
(C) Creating advertisements
(D) Using a device

8. According to the conversation, what will happen this afternoon?
(A) Some equipment will be delivered.
(B) A colleague will leave early.
(C) A repair person will visit.
(D) Some software will be installed.

Listen to a short talk, and choose the best answer to each question.

9. Who most likely is the speaker?
(A) A theater producer
(B) A tour guide
(C) A hotel manager
(D) An airline official

10. What is included as part of the special package?
(A) Tickets to a museum
(B) A map of the city
(C) A meal at a restaurant
(D) Transportation into town

11. What are staff members asked to do?
(A) Offer customers upgrades
(B) Learn about an exhibit
(C) Try a menu item
(D) Hand brochures to customers

☑ **TIPS-9**

Who 設問＝「職業」！
⇒Who 設問では、職業
　や職種が問われる

□ official　役員

☑ **TIPS-10**

キーワードを待ち伏せ！
⇒設問の名詞キーワード
　(special package)
　を耳印にする

□ meal　食事
□ transportation
　移動

☑ **TIPS-11**

ask 問題＝「お願い」！
⇒ask問題は、説明文後
　半の「お願い」「指示」
　を聞く

□ customer　顧客
□ exhibit　展覧会
□ brochure
　パンフレット

Choose the best answer to complete the sentence.

12. Employees who ------- to take time off in August are asked to let their supervisor know as soon as possible.

(A) intend
(B) intention
(C) intentionally
(D) internal

✓ **TIPS-12**

選択肢の品詞がバラバラ→品詞問題！
⇒空所の品詞を見抜けば即答

□ intend to do
　〜するつもり
□ supervisor　上司

13. In April, the company received ------- to construct a new store on Brady Street.

(A) approve
(B) approval
(C) approving
(D) approvingly

✓ **TIPS-13 & -14**

文のカタチをチェック！
⇒13「receive＋（目的語＝名詞）」、14「a＋（形容詞）＋N」

□ construct
　〜を建設する
□ approve
　〜を承認する
□ workmate
　仕事仲間
□ environment　環境

14. On her last day, Ms. Hope thanked her workmates for providing a ------- environment.

(A) support
(B) supporter
(C) supportively
(D) supportive

15. The guide spoke ------- about the factory's processes to the group of investors.

(A) information
(B) informatively
(C) informative
(D) inform

✓ **TIPS-15**

「V＋副」のパターン！

□ process　工程
□ investor　投資家

16. A ------- survey was used to find ways in which the online store could improve its services.

(A) satisfy
(B) satisfied
(C) satisfaction
(D) satisfactorily

✓ **TIPS-16**

「N＋N」が出る！
⇒「a＋（ ）＋N」では、空所＝形容詞とは限らない

□ survey　調査
□ online store　オンラインストア
□ improve　〜を改善・向上させる

Choose the best answer to complete the text.
Questions 17-20 refer to the following article.

Travel — Tokyo

-------- Tokyo has long been one of the world's major centers of fashion,
17.
finance, and art. ----------, its suitability as a tourist destination has been
18.
comparatively overlooked. In recent years this is changing. For people
looking for something truly different, Tokyo is an exciting option. High-
technology and ancient tradition exist alongside each other in a wonderful
harmony, -------- that it has something to offer everyone. There are plentiful
19.
first-class accommodation and excellent food from all over the world.
Furthermore, world-class ski fields are only a short flight away. Tokyo is
-------- a city worth considering for your next family holiday.
20.

☐ suitability　適合性
☐ destination
　目的地
☐ comparatively
　比較的に
☐ overlook
　～を見落とす
☐ ancient tradition
　古くからの伝統
☐ alongside each
　other　互いに並んで
☐ accommodation
　宿泊施設

17. (A) Tokyo's attractiveness to travelers is not what it once was.
　　(B) Tokyo is a wonderful travel destination that is becoming more and
　　　　more affordable.
　　(C) Tokyo is a city focused on industry and finance with little to
　　　　offer travelers.
　　(D) Tokyo should be avoided in favor of other towns such as Osaka
　　　　and Nagoya.

☑ **TIPS-17**

文選択問題は難問！
⇒空所前後や語句の関
　連性にヒントを探そ
　う

☐ attractiveness
　魅力
☐ avoid　～を避ける

18. (A) As a result
　　(B) Similarly
　　(C) Yet
　　(D) For example

☑ **TIPS-18**

ロジックで解く！
⇒接続詞問題では、空
　所前後のロジックを
　見る

19. (A) meaning
　　(B) meaningful
　　(C) meaningfully
　　(D) mean

20. (A) nearly
　　(B) hardly
　　(C) fairly
　　(D) certainly

☑ **TIPS-20**

消去法を活用して！
⇒語句問題は知らない
　と解けない

Choose the best answer for each question.

Questions 21-22 refer to the following advertisement.

Brandon International Schools (BIS)

BIS provides education for students aged six through 18 in many locations around the world. We are looking for adventurous people with valid teaching credentials to work in locations such as Mauritius, Papua New Guinea, the Seychelles, and the Galapagos Islands.

BIS offers you a chance to get valuable teaching experience necessary to obtain a dream position in an elite private institution. Positions at BIS are well paid and you will receive support from a capable management team with years of experience. BIS even pays for one trip back to your home country each year so that you may spend your holiday with family members.

Learn more about the positions we have available and read about the experiences of our past and present employees by visiting the Web page at www.bischools.org. If you would like to make an inquiry or apply for a position, contact us at hr@bischools.org.

---

21. What is a benefit of working for BIS?

(A) High remuneration
(B) Long holidays
(C) Free accommodation
(D) Subsidized training opportunities

22. How should interested people contact BIS?

(A) By visiting the Web site
(B) By calling a school
(C) By visiting the offices
(D) By sending an e-mail

□ adventurous 冒険好きな
□ credential 免許状
□ private institution 私立学校
□ well paid 給与がいい
□ make an inquiry 問い合わせる
□ apply for 〜に応募する

✓ TIPS-21

「条件」をサーチ！
⇒求人では、ポストに関する条件が問われる

□ remuneration 報酬
□ subsidized 助成された
□ opportunity 機会

✓ TIPS-22

連絡手段は文末！

□ contact 〜に連絡する

Choose the best answer for each question.
Questions 23-24 refer to the following message.

While you were out

To: Steve Orta
From: Freda Hale
Time: 3:00, Wednesday

Message:
Freda Hale from Hale Hardware dropped by. She was on her way Ling's Chinese Restaurant and she wanted to see if you were free for lunch. She mentioned that she was expecting to receive the designs for the extensions to their shop sometime this week. She has a small change she wants to discuss with you before you print them out. Can you give her a call before you leave today?
Message received by: Wendy Noskoff

23. Why did Ms. Hale visit Mr. Orta's office?
(A) To collect some designs
(B) To remind Mr. Orta of a deadline
(C) To attend an information session
(D) To discuss a colleague

24. What will Mr. Orta probably do?
(A) Read a report
(B) Check a Web site
(C) Call a client
(D) Buy some equipment

☐ drop by　訪問する
☐ on one's way
　　途中
☐ extension
　　拡張、増築
☐ give one's a call
～に電話する

✓ **TIPS-23**

メッセージの目的は冒頭!
⇒訪問や電話の目的は、最初の数行にヒント

☐ remind
　　～に気づかせる
☐ deadline　締め切り
☐ information
　　session　説明会

✓ **TIPS-24**

will do→文末にヒント!
⇒will do は「今後の展開」問題。文末のお願い表現を見よう

TOEIC テストの「リスニング」は、すべてを聞こうとしてはダメです。設問を先読みし、何が問われているかをチェックしましょう。設問のキーワード（名詞）は耳印になります。

part 1

 6

Look at the picture and choose the statment that best describes what you see.

1. (A) (B) (C) (D)

2. (A) (B) (C) (D)

☑ **TIPS-1**

「影」が出る！
⇒建物の影にも目を向けて

☐ rooftop　屋上
☐ traffic light　信号
☐ sidewalk　歩道
☐ be cast
　　（影が）投げかけられる

☑ **TIPS-2**

歩く「方向」をチェック！
⇒人物や車の移動方向が出る

☐ pedestrian　歩行者
☐ in opposite direction
　　反対方向に
☐ dine　食事をする

Choose the best response to each question or statement.

3. (A) (B) (C)

4. (A) (B) (C)

5. (A) (B) (C)

☑ **TIPS**

Yes/No にこだわるな！
⇒ Are you~? Do you~?
に対し、Yes/No が
正解とは限らない

☐ banquet　宴会
☐ operate　～を操作す
る

part**3** 8

Listen to a short conversation, and choose the best answer to each question.

6. What does the woman ask the men to do?
(A) Go shopping for some stationary
(B) Help carry some documents
(C) Repair some equipment
(D) Interview a job candidate

7. What will most likely happen tomorrow?
(A) The men will visit a client.
(B) A construction project will start.
(C) A banquet will be held.
(D) The woman will give a presentation.

8. What does Trevor agree to do?
(A) Go to the warehouse
(B) Buy some supplies
(C) Bring some tools
(D) Call Wendy

☑ **TIPS-6**

ask 問題！
⇒女性の「お願い」は
何？

☐ stationery　文房具
☐ document　書類
☐ repair　～を修理する
☐ job candidate
求職者

☑ **TIPS-7**

「予定」をつかめ！
⇒女性の明日の予定
は？

☐ client　顧客
☐ construction project
建築計画
☐ give a presentation
プレゼンを行う

☑ **TIPS-8**

Trevor の後を聞こう！
⇒男性二人のパターンで
は、二人目（Trevor）
が何をするかがポイ
ント

☐ warehouse　倉庫
☐ tool　道具

Listen to a short talk, and choose the best answer to each question.

9. What is the news report mainly about?
(A) A new stadium
(B) A local festival
(C) A government initiative
(D) An amusement park

10. What does Kilgore hope to attract?
(A) Tourists
(B) Academic visitors
(C) Business investors
(D) Entertainers

11. What does the speaker mean when he says, "This is where it might face problems"?
(A) The plan is not very popular.
(B) People do not want to attract tourists.
(C) Kilgore is far from any major attractions.
(D) People are worried about the cost.

☑ TIPS-9

主題は冒頭！
⇒ニュースの基本パ
　ターン

□ initiative　発議

☑ TIPS-10

プロジェクトの対象は
誰？
⇒プロジェクト＝観光
　と分かれば簡単

□ investor　投資者
□ entertainer　芸人

☑ TIPS-11

ターゲット文（" "）を耳
印に！
⇒ターゲット文を含む
　問題では前後関係を
　つかもう

□ attract tourist　旅行
　者を魅了する
□ far from ～から遠い

Choose the best answer to complete the sentence.

12. It is the ------- of the night manager to ensure the all of the restaurant's doors and windows are locked before leaving.

(A) responsibility
(B) responsibly
(C) response
(D) responsible

☑ **TIPS-12**

「the+(名)」！
⇒品詞問題。意味でなく、カタチから解こう

☐ ensure
　　～確実にする
☐ lock　～を施錠する

13. At the end of the building's construction, any ------- materials will be sent to a recycling plant.

(A) remain
(B) remaining
(C) remainder
(D) remains

☑ **TIPS-13**

「any ＋(形)＋N」！
⇒品詞問題。形容詞＝分詞に気づけば簡単

☐ construction　建設
☐ material　資材
☐ recycling plant
　　リサイクル工場

14. Mr. Slater was sure that the company's sales goals would be ------- by as early as September.

(A) achievement
(B) achiever
(C) achieve
(D) achievable

☑ **TIPS-14**

「be動詞＋(形容詞／分詞)」！

☐ sales goal　売上目標
☐ as early as　早くも

15. Every year, during the holiday season, products are displayed ------- in the store's windows.

(A) creative
(B) creatively
(C) creation
(D) create

☑ **TIPS-15**

「受け身」を見抜け！
⇒品詞問題。受け身be displayedなので、空所に名詞は×

☐ be displayed　陳列される

16. Renters of vehicles must ------- with the terms and conditions outlined in the rental agreement.

(A) compliant
(B) compliance
(C) comply
(D) compliantly

☑ **TIPS-16**

「助動詞＋(動詞の原型)」！

☐ renters of vehicles
　　レンタカー業者
☐ terms and conditions
　　取引条件
☐ rental agreement
　　賃貸契約書

Choose the best answer to complete the text.
Questions 17-20 refer to the following notice.

NOTICE

All staff at Normandy Research Laboratory are -------- to take part
17.
in a safety workshop. Government regulations require that you fully
understand and follow certain safety procedures and reporting protocols.
It will be impossible to have every staff member attend the workshop at
the same time. -------- The first workshop will be on Friday, December 3.
18.
A second workshop will be held on Monday, December 6. If you would
like to attend both, please ask your -------- supervisor for permission. If
19.
for any reason, you are unable to attend either of the -------- , you will be
20.
required to attend one at the Department of Industry and Commerce at
235 Robert Street.

---

17. (A) allowed
 (B) attended
 (C) concerned
 (D) required

18. (A) For that reason, we are offering it twice.
 (B) Nevertheless, you are invited to join.
 (C) There will be no other opportunities.
 (D) So, the event has been canceled this year.

19. (A) responsive
 (B) approximate
 (C) immediate
 (D) reasonable

20. (A) rehearsals
 (B) sessions
 (C) institutions
 (D) attractions

□ take part in ～に参
加する
□ regulation 規定
□ safety procedure
安全手順
□ protocol 協定
□ supervisor 上司
□ permission 許可

☑ **TIPS-17**

定型文が出る！
⇒「be ( ) to do」(～が
求められる)は？

☑ **TIPS-18**

空所後のfirstとsecond
をチェック！
⇒文選択問題。空所前後
にヒントがある

□ nevertheless それ
にもかかわらず
□ opportunity 機会

☑ **TIPS-19**

フレーズを見抜け！
⇒「( ) supervisor」
(直属の上司)は？

☑ **TIPS-20**

言い換えが出る！
⇒workshopを言い換
えると？

Choose the best answer for each question.
Questions 21-22 refer to the following test chain.

ROD MATHERS   8:50 A.M.

I'm running a bit late this morning. Can you ask them to delay the start of the planning meeting?

CHRISTIE TANAKA   8:51 A.M.

I will, but can you give me a reason?

ROD MATHERS   8:53 A.M.

I'm stuck in a traffic jam. There's no telling how long it'll take.

CHRISTIE TANAKA   8:53 A.M.

OK. I'll let the others know. Give me a call if you have an update.

ROD MATHERS   8:54 A.M.

Sure. If I'm not there by 10:00, you can start without me.

CHRISTIE TANAKA   8:59 A.M.

We were counting on you to open the meeting with a presentation on the survey results, though.

ROD MATHERS   9:02 A.M.

Brad Walters has all of that information, so I'm sure he can take my place.

CHRISTIE TANAKA   9:03 A.M.

I'll let him know to be ready.

---

21. At 8:53 A.M., what does Mr. Mathers mean when he writes, "There's no telling how long it'll take"?

(A) He does not know when he will arrive.
(B) He cannot share some confidential information.
(C) He is not aware of the meeting schedule.
(D) He was not involved in the planning committee.

22. Why will the woman contact Mr. Walters?

(A) To send him a survey
(B) To offer him a promotion
(C) To learn about a traffic situation
(D) To ask him to open a meeting

□ delay ～を遅らせる
□ traffic jam 交通渋滞
□ count on ～を当てにする
□ survey results 調査結果

☑ TIPS-21

ターゲット文（" "）の前を見よう！
⇒直前のtraffic jamにヒント

□ confidential information 秘密情報
□ be aware of ～に気づく
□ be involved in ～に関わる
□ planning committee 企画委員会

☑ TIPS-22

主題を見抜く！
⇒女性のセリフを辿って、主題を見つけよう

□ promotion 昇進
□ traffic situation 交通状況

Choose the best answer for each question.

Questions 23-24 refer to the following notice.

Notice to Thorne City Residents

From August 1, the council will begin enforcing a code which applies to landowners. The council guidelines state that fences and walls between neighboring properties must be a maximum of two meters tall. It appears that some residents have been creating barriers in excess of that height. From August 1, members of the council code enforcement section will be going from house to house measuring wall and fence heights. The owners of walls and fences in excess of the official height will be issued warnings and asked to comply within two months. If you would like to schedule a meeting with a representative to discuss exceptions, learn more about council codes, or see a list of council approved fence builders, visit the Web site at www.thornecc.org/residentialcodes.

---

23. What is the purpose of the notice?

(A) To advertise employment opportunities at the city council
(B) To inform people that inspections will be carried out
(C) To announce the outcome of a vote
(D) To request assistance with data collection

24. What is NOT available on the Web site?

(A) Appointment scheduling
(B) Details of regulations
(C) Landscaping advice
(D) A list of construction companies

☐ council　議会
☐ enforce
　　〜を実施する
☐ code　規定
☐ landowner
　　土地所有者
☐ property　土地
☐ resident　住民
☐ barrier　障壁
☐ warning　警告
☐ comply　従う
☐ representative
　　代表者

✓ **TIPS-23**

お知らせの目的は冒頭！
⇒前半から「法施行→(壁
　の)計測」を読み取る

☐ advertise　〜を宣伝
　　する
☐ city council　市議会
☐ inspection　調査
☐ outcome　結果
☐ data collection
　　データ収集

✓ **TIPS-24**

NOT問題を攻略！
⇒Web siteをヒント
　に、本文と選択肢を比
　較検討する

☐ regulation　規定
☐ landscaping　風景、
　　展望

TOEICテストの「リーディング」は、スピーディな処理能力が求められます。Part5は1問20秒、Part6&7は1問1分が標準時間。設問を先にチェックして、早く解くことが大事です。

part 1 10

Look at the picture and choose the statment that best describes what you see.

1. (A) (B) (C) (D)

2.(A) (B) (C) (D)

part2 11

Choose the best response to each question or statement.

3. (A) (B) (C)

4. (A) (B) (C)

5. (A) (B) (C)

☑ **TIPS**

付加疑問文の文末は無
視しよう！

☐ committee　委員会
☐ competitive　競争的
な
☐ by the door　ドアの
そば

part3 12

Listen to a short conversation, and choose the best answer to each
question.

6. What event does the woman want to attend?

(A) A museum exhibition
(B) A concert
(C) A play
(D) A sporting competition

☑ **TIPS-6**

選択肢をタテ読み！
⇒選択肢をざっと見て、
　イベントの種類をイ
　メージしよう

☐ exhibition　展覧会
☐ competition　競技会

7. What does the man say about tonight's event?

(A) It has been canceled.
(B) It will be attended by a special guest.
(C) It was advertised on the radio.
(D) It will start an hour late.

☑ **TIPS-7**

キーワードが耳印！
⇒キーワードtonight's
　eventを待ち伏せ

☐ special guest　特別
ゲスト
☐ advertise　〜を宣伝
する

8. What does the woman mean when she says, "I'll look forward to it,
then"?

(A) She respects a performer.
(B) She will wait for more information.
(C) She expects to receive a program.
(D) She will watch a film.

☑ **TIPS-8**

ターゲット文("　")の意
図を見抜こう。
⇒意図問題。何を期待し
　ているのかをつかむ

☐ performer　出演者
☐ receive　〜を受け取
る

Listen to a short talk, and choose the best answer to each question.

9. Why is the speaker calling?
(A) To ask for a schedule update
(B) To request some paperwork
(C) To remind an employee of a meeting
(D) To thank a supplier for some assistance

10. What is scheduled for Friday afternoon?
(A) A picnic
(B) A sales event
(C) A delivery
(D) A party

11. What does the speaker mean when she says, "That one's not so pressing"?
(A) An event is not very important.
(B) Some guests will arrive late.
(C) Production has not begun yet.
(D) A task is not urgent.

☑ **TIPS-9**

電話の用件は？
⇒冒頭で述べられるの
　がセオリー

☐ schedule update
　スケジュールの更新
☐ paperwork　事務処理
☐ remind A of B　Aに
　Bを確認する
☐ supplier　発注先

☑ **TIPS-10**

イベントを予測！
⇒選択肢を「タテ」読み
　して、音を待ち伏せし
　よう

☑ **TIPS-11**

言い換えに反応！
⇒pressingの言い換え
　が分かればOK

☐ pressing　緊急の

Choose the best answer to complete the sentence.

12. The new president of GHJ Enterprises ------- into the position last month.

(A) was voted
(B) is voting
(C) voted
(D) votes

13. Mr. Sales ------- the selection committee with his excellent credentials and agreeable character.

(A) was impressed
(B) impressed
(C) is impressed
(D) to impress

14. Factory managers ------- that they may need to replace many aging machines in the next few months.

(A) concern
(B) are concerning
(C) will concern
(D) are concerned

15. The cost of building supplies ------- three-fold in the last 20 years.

(A) has been increased
(B) has increased
(C) increases
(D) was increased

16. Brian Doors ------- as one of the most knowledgeable authors on Internet Marketing in the UK.

(A) regards
(B) is regarding
(C) is regarded
(D) has regarded

Choose the best answer to complete the text.
Questions 17-20 refer to the following e-mail.

To:	Joan Chang <jchang@harperlaw.com>
From:	Phil Miller <pmiller@harperlaw.com>
Date:	April 6
Subject:	Expansion

Hi Joan,

Having recently taken on some new clients, I think it is time for us to hire new staff. Of course, our current office is already at capacity so we need to look at renting a new office suite. I -------- we should look
17.
for something a little closer to town but not too central. -------- Her
18.
name is Rebecca Horne and she is in charge of commercial real-estate there. Her e-mail address is rhorne@haliburtonr.com. She is very familiar with our business needs. Please explain that we will need at least four more -------- than we currently have.
19.

Let me know when you have a short list of locations. We can go and ---
-------- them together sometime next week.
20.

Best,
Phil Miller

□ current office 現在のオフィス
□ be in charge of ～の担当である
□ commercial real-estate 商業用物件

☑ **TIPS-17**

選択肢の品詞がバラバラ！
⇒品詞問題。空所の品詞が分かればOK

☑ **TIPS-18**

空所の後を見よ！
⇒文選択問題。空所後のHer nameがヒント

□ agent 代理人
□ foreseeable 予知できる
□ appreciate ～を感謝する
□ tenant 借用者

☑ **TIPS-19**

「物件」の別名は？
⇒文脈問題。何を探しているかをつかむ

17. (A) believable
(B) believer
(C) belief
(D) believe

18. (A) I would like you to contact an agent from Haliburton Realty.
(B) This office should be adequate for the foreseeable future.
(C) Please inform them that we appreciate the opportunity to serve them.
(D) We cannot afford to have unhappy tenants.

19. (A) clients
(B) suppliers
(C) rooms
(D) holidays

20. (A) interview
(B) inspect
(C) solve
(D) arrange

☑ TIPS-20

「行って見る」は？
⇒We can go and (　)
　は定型文

part 7

Choose the best answer for each question.
Questions 21-23 refer to the following Web page.

---

http://infocusphotographers.com

In Focus Photographers

In Focus Photographers (IFP) is a directory of professional photographers from every part of the country. People looking to hire a photographer for a single job or even on a regular basis can register for free and obtain unlimited access to our directory. Each photographer's portfolio and contact details are available so that potential clients can contact them directly and negotiate a price, a small share of which is payable to IFP.

Additionally, we have an online bidding service, whereby potential clients can post a job description and interested photographers can offer their services.

To ensure that only the most capable and reliable photographers are registered with the service, we use a rating and review system that allows past clients to comment on the quality of the service. Photographers with a rating lower than four stars are restricted from bidding on projects until a formal review has been conducted.

☐ directory 　人名鑑
☐ on a regular basis
　定期的に
☐ register 　～に登録す
　る
☐ potential clients 　見
　込み客
☐ negotiate a price
　料金の交渉をする
☐ payable 　～に支払わ
　れる
☐ bidding 　入札
☐ restrict 　～を制限す
　る

21. What is NOT part of the IFP service?

(A) Providing contact details of photographers
(B) Allowing photographers to submit offers for work
(C) Displaying samples of photographers' work
(D) Renting photography equipment to professionals

☑ TIPS-21

ＮＯＴ問題はハイレベ
ル！
⇒選択肢を見て、本文の
　該当箇所をサーチ

☐ photography
　equipment 　写真機材

22. How does IFP generate income?

(A) It receives a commission from photographers.
(B) It charges users a registration fee.
(C) It posts advertisements from equipment manufacturers.
(D) It charges members to attend special events.

☑ TIPS-22

利益はどこから？
⇒priceやpayableなど
　のマネーワードにヒント

☐ commission 　手数料
☐ charge （料金を）請
　求する
☐ registration fee 　登
　録料
☐ post 　～を掲載する
☐ manufacturer 　メー
　カー

23. What happens to photographers with unsatisfactory ratings?

(A) They are removed from the directory.
(B) They are asked to refund payment.
(C) Their clients are interviewed.
(D) Their work is audited.

Choose the best answer for each question.
Questions 24-25 refer to the following form.

Strident Online Store
Product Return Form

Dear Customer,

Strident Online Store takes great pride in its selection of only the best fashion accessories and timepieces for its catalog. Nevertheless, it is inevitable that some goods do not operate to the high standards we expect. If you are not entirely satisfied with your order, please feel free to send it back and request a replacement or a refund. We only ask that you provide a description of the problem you experienced so that we can ensure that it does not happen again.

Name: Georgia Singh
Address: 45 Herman Road, Hobart, TAS 7004
Description of the problem: It was fine for the first couple of days, but it seems to be a little slow. I think the battery needs replacing or there is something wrong with the mechanism.

---

24. What product did Ms. Singh most likely buy?

(A) A computer
(B) A watch
(C) An appliance
(D) A toy

25. What problem is Ms. Singh reporting?

(A) An incorrect item
(B) A late delivery
(C) A malfunction
(D) A missing part

☑ **TIPS-23**

ネガティブ・ワードを探せ！
⇒unsatisfactory ratingsの言い換えがポイント

☐ unsatisfactory　不満足な
☐ refund payment　返金する
☐ audit　～を監査する

☐ take pride in　～を誇りに思う
☐ timepiece　時計
☐ inevitable　不可欠な
☐ replacement　交換
☐ description　説明

☑ **TIPS-24**

商品をチェック！
⇒オンラインストアの商品は冒頭を見よう

☐ appliance　電気製品
☐ toy　おもちゃ

☑ **TIPS-25**

何のクレームかを把握して！
⇒後半に商品の「問題」と「解決策」が記載

☐ malfunction　故障

【文選択問題】(Part6)　選択肢 1 ～ 4 から本文に挿入する文章を選ぶ問題です。
空所前後の流れ（展開）を見極める必要があります。代名詞や接続副詞がヒント
になります。

part**1** 14

Look at the picture and choose the statement that best describes what
you see.

1. (A) (B) (C) (D)

(A) (B) (C) (D)

☑ **TIPS-1**

動作をキャッチ！
⇒Part1のセオリー。難
　単語はスルーでも解け
　る

☐ wheelbarrow　手押
　し車
☐ adjust　～を調整する
☐ step on ～に乗る
☐ dirt　土

☑ **TIPS-2**

主語がバラバラ→難
問！
⇒消去法を使って、正答
　率を上げよう

☐ be lined up　整列す
　る
☐ lawn　芝生
☐ curb　縁石

part2   15

Choose the best response to each question or statement.

3. (A) (B) (C)

4. (A) (B) (C)

5. (A) (B) (C)

☑ **TIPS**

トリッキーな応答！
⇒例えば、「注文した？」
　に対し、「マークに聞い
　てみる」という応答が
　出る

part3   16

Listen to a short conversation, and choose the best answer to each question.

6. What will happen on Monday morning?

(A) A policy will take effect.
(B) A new employee will start work.
(C) A sales campaign will kick off.
(D) A new product will go on sale.

7. What will be delivered this afternoon?

(A) Artwork
(B) Food
(C) Stationery
(D) Furniture

8. What does the woman ask the man to do?

(A) Attend a training workshop
(B) Prepare a speech
(C) Watch an instructional video
(D) Prepare a computer

☑ **TIPS-6**

キーワード＝耳印！
⇒キーワードMonday
　morningから、トピッ
　クを見抜く

☐ take effect　効力を
　発する
☐ kick off　始める
☐ go on sale　発売され
　る

☑ **TIPS-7**

deskを言い換えると？
⇒「机」「椅子」の上位語

☐ artwork　美術作品
☐ furniture　家具

☑ **TIPS-8**

「お願い」をキャッチ！
⇒ask問題。(女性の)お
　願い文Can you〜？に
　ヒント

☐ instructional video
　説明ビデオ

Listen to a short talk, and choose the best answer to each question.

9. What is implied about Vendura Technologies?

(A) It is changing its name.
(B) It manufactures office equipment.
(C) It is merging with the speaker's company.
(D) It develops software for communications.

10. What does the speaker imply when he says, "March is sooner than you think"?

(A) The company is always busy at this time of year.
(B) They have not checked the calendar.
(C) There is an important sale coming up.
(D) They do not have much time to prepare.

11. What can interested people receive from the speaker?

(A) An invitation to a workshop
(B) A ticket for an event
(C) An introduction to an expert
(D) An instruction manual

☑ **TIPS-9**

会社説明は冒頭！
⇒名詞から、どんな会社
か（会社の業種）をイ
メージする

☐ manufacture 〜 ？
製造する
☐ merge with 〜と ？
併する

☑ **TIPS-10**

逆発想しよう！
⇒March is sooner(3月
はすぐ)を言い換える
と？

☑ **TIPS-11**

receive←→give！
⇒「受け取る」と「与え
る」の関係がヒント

☐ invitation 招待状
☐ introduction 紹介
☐ instruction manua ？
取扱説明書

Choose the best answer to complete the sentence.

12. Since the new office was opened in June, we ------- about 10 additional staff members.

(A) have hired
(B) hire
(C) are hiring
(D) were hired

13. At next week's building material exposition in Paris, Mr. Collins ------- a supplier who is offering big discounts on important supplies.

(A) met
(B) will meet
(C) had been met
(D) has met

14. Ms. Chambers ------- to submit her travel report as soon as she got back to the office.

(A) is asking
(B) has asked
(C) will be asked
(D) was asked

15. The office manager is using one of the company vehicles until his car -------.

(A) is being repaired
(B) is repaired
(C) is repairing
(D) was repaired

16. Phil Orta has announced that he ------- after the GHT Model smartphone is released in June.

(A) has retired
(B) is retired
(C) will retire
(D) was retiring

☑ **TIPS-12&13**

「時」のキーワードを見つけよう！
⇒Sinceならば「完了形」、at the next weekならば「未来形」

☐ additional staff　追加スタッフ
☐ exposition　展示会
☐ offer discounts　割引を提示する

☑ **TIPS-14**

時制の一致！
⇒文後半のshe got backがヒント

☑ **TIPS-15**

受け身を攻略！
⇒空所の前がhis carなので、「受け身」を疑うのがセオリー

☐ vehicle　乗物

☑ **TIPS-16**

before/afterに反応しよう！
⇒空所後のafterを見て、「未来」をイメージ

Choose the best answer to complete the text.
Questions 17-20 refer to the following notice.

Thank you for registering as a --------- of Primovision Online. You are
17.
now able to download and watch television dramas, documentaries,
and feature-length movies from our library to watch on a wide range of
Internet-connected devices. As you have --------- out the basic plan, you
18.
are entitled to watch up to 20 hours of content each month. --------- It is
19.
even possible to upgrade for a set number of months, after which your
membership will automatically return to the basic plan. Billing ---------- on
20.
the fifteenth of each month. If you cancel your membership mid-month,
the remaining portion will be refunded by bank transfer.

---

17. (A) reviewer
    (B) provider
    (C) consultant
    (D) customer

18. (A) taken
    (B) filled
    (C) moved
    (D) found

19. (A) Please submit films according to our published guidelines.
    (B) However, you will be given another chance to apply next month.
    (C) You can upgrade to the Standard Plan or Premium Plan at any
        time.
    (D) You have paid for a full year in advance.

20. (A) occurred
    (B) will occur
    (C) has occurred
    (D) is occurred

☐ feature-length movi
　長編映画
☐ be entitled to do
　～する権利がある
☐ membership　会員
☐ billing　請求
☐ remaining portion
　残りの分
☐ bank transfer　銀行
　振替

✓ TIPS-17

「顧客」への文書が出
る！
⇒（講読等の）規約や取
　扱説明書などは定番

✓ TIPS-18

柔軟な発想を持とう！
⇒「～を連れ出す」の
　ニュアンス

✓ TIPS-19

アップグレードの文脈！
⇒文選択問題。空所後で
　は「（プランを）変えて
　も、ベーシックに戻
　る」とある

☐ pay for　支払う
☐ in advance　前も
　て

✓ TIPS-20

請求は「これから」！
⇒空所前後の文は、will
　を使った未来形

Choose the best answer for each question.
Questions 21-23 refer to the following Web page.

http://www.museumcuratorinsider.com

Welcome to the Web site of *Museum Curator Insider*
Special Offer

Museum Curator Insider is a quarterly magazine for museum employees to learn about the latest technologies and trends in exhibition planning and promotion. It also has interviews with the curators of the world's top art galleries and museums as well as experts in presentation and preservation. As it is an industry journal, *Museum Curator Insider* is tax deductible in most regions.

Unfortunately, trial subscriptions are no longer available. However, please click here if you would like to read a sample issue from last year.

The publication is currently offered in English, French, German, Japanese, and Spanish and can be shipped to as many as 36 different countries. International shipping rates apply. More information about that is available during the ordering process. Be sure to indicate which language you require. Otherwise, the English version will be shipped automatically.

Institutions registered with the International Federation of Historical Conservation are eligible to get five percent off the price of each issue.

21. How often is *Museum Curator Insider* published?

(A) Once a week
(B) Once a month
(C) Once every three months
(D) Once every six months

22. What is NOT implied about *Museum Curator Insider*?

(A) It can be delivered internationally.
(B) It contains information about caring for artifacts.
(C) It is available in multiple languages.
(D) It features advertisements.

23. How can institutions get a discount subscription?

(A) By subscribing for more than 12 months
(B) By joining a union of organizations
(C) By ordering multiple copies of each issue
(D) By contributing articles to the magazine

□ quarterly magazine　季刊誌
□ latest　最新の
□ curator　学芸員
□ tax deductible　税金を控除できる
□ trial subscription　お試し講読
□ currently　現在
□ shipping rate　配送料金
□ be eligible to do　～する資格がある

✓ **TIPS-21**

出版の「頻度」！
⇒quarterlyがヒント

✓ **TIPS-22**

選択肢をシンプルに捉える！
⇒NOT問題。(A)発送、(B)美術品、(C)言語、(D)広告。ざっくり捉えてから、本文をサーチ

□ artifact　美術品
□ multiple　複数の
□ feature　～を特集する

✓ **TIPS-23**

割引は文末！
⇒five percentなどの数が目印。文末を読もう

□ institution　機関
□ subscribe　～を講読する
□ each issue　各号
□ contribute A to B　AをBに寄稿する

【テキストメッセージ＆チャット】（Part7）　複数の人物がメッセージをやり取りしている画面が出題されます。会話を読む感じなので、LINEをイメージすると簡単です。

part 1　 18

Look at the picture and choose the statement that best describes what you see.

1. (A) (B) (C) (D)

2.(A) (B) (C) (D)

☑ TIPS-1

「水面」の建物が出る！
⇒例えばThe buildings overlook the river.
（建物から川が見渡せる）

□ vessel　船
□ be covered with
　　～で覆われている
□ waterway　運河

☑ TIPS-2

「席」の状態を見よ！
⇒レストランでは、席が「空いているか」「埋まっているか」がポイント

□ patron　客
□ be stacked
　　積み上げられている
□ sunshade　日よけ

Choose the best response to each question or statement.

3. (A) (B) (C)

4. (A) (B) (C)

5. (A) (B) (C)

Listen to a short conversation, and choose the best answer to each question.

6. What are the speakers mainly discussing?

(A) Hiring entertainers
(B) Ordering food
(C) Carrying out repairs
(D) Finding a venue

7. What most likely is the problem?

(A) Some equipment is broken.
(B) Some guests are unavailable.
(C) A delivery fee is too expensive.
(D) A business is closed.

8. What will the man most likely do next?

(A) Order some furniture
(B) Call a client
(C) Request a catalog
(D) Reschedule an event

☑ **TIPS**

提案・勧誘は頻出！
⇒Why don't you〜?
（〜してはどうですか）
などは「提案」の定番

☐ organize a banquet
　宴席を設ける
☐ breakroom　休憩室

☑ **TIPS-6**

忘年会（パーティ）の細
部を聞こう

☐ entertainer　芸人
☐ venue　会場

☑ **TIPS-7**

具体的なトラブル・不備
が出る

☐ unavailable　手があ
　いていない
☐ delivery fee　配送料
　金

☑ **TIPS-8**

do next→「次の展開」！
⇒会話終盤のI' ll〜にヒ
ント

☐ furniture　家具
☐ reschedule　（計画を）
　変更する

Listen to a short talk, and choose the best answer to each question.

9. What does the speaker talk about on her radio program?

(A) Business news
(B) Gardening tips
(C) Financial advice
(D) Music reviews

10. What does the speaker say about Higgs Industries' new product?

(A) It is durable.
(B) It is made locally.
(C) It has won an award.
(D) It is affordable.

11. According to the speaker, what can listeners find on the Higgs Industries Web site?

(A) Discount offers
(B) Warranty information
(C) An order form
(D) Product applications

☑ **TIPS-9**

番組の趣旨は何？
⇒セオリー通り、冒頭に
　集中

☐ financial　財政的な
☐ review　批評

☑ **TIPS-10**

名詞キーワードの後を
聞け！
⇒Higgs Industriesの
　直後がヒント

☐ durable　丈夫な
☐ win an award　賞を
　受賞する
☐ affordable　入手可能な

☑ **TIPS-11**

ウェブ情報が出る！
⇒追加情報や補足は終
　盤を聞こう

☐ warranty　保証
☐ application　用途

Choose the best answer to complete the sentence.

12. Mr. Kato ------- several restaurants on Tudor Street whenever he stays in London on business.

(A) frequents
(B) frequently
(C) frequent
(D) frequency

✓ TIPS-12

選択肢の品詞がバラバラ！
⇒品詞問題。空所の後の品詞がヒント

☐ frequent　しばしば

13. In his yearly speech, the company president pointed out that every department in the company is ------- important.

(A) equal
(B) equally
(C) equality
(D) equaled

✓ TIPS-13

形容詞を修飾するのは？
⇒[be動詞＋（　　）＋形容詞]

☐ point out　指摘する

14. According to the airline's Web site, it takes ------- three hours to fly from Brisbane to Perth.

(A) approximation
(B) approximate
(C) approximating
(D) approximately

✓ TIPS-14

「およそ」3時間！
⇒空所＝aboutの副詞

☐ According to
　～によれば

15. Both Garland Industries and Jeffries Corporation ------- medical equipment under government contracts.

(A) productively
(B) produce
(C) production
(D) productive

✓ TIPS-15

動詞の有無をチェック！
⇒[S＋（　　）＋O]

☐ medical equipment
　医療器具
☐ contract　契約

16. Managers at McLachlan Restaurants seldom ------- kitchen staff before an inspection is carried out.

(A) informative
(B) informatively
(C) inform
(D) information

✓ TIPS-16

seldomに惑わされるな！
⇒[S＋seldom＋（　）＋O]

☐ seldom　めったに～ない
☐ inspection　検査

Choose the best answer to complete the text.
Questions 17-20 refer to the following article.

Blair Valley Selling Fast

Bradford's latest housing development to go on sale is Blair Valley and house and land packages there are selling at a surprising --------- It has **17.** only been a week since the properties went on sale and more than half have been bought. According to the developer, this is because of the excellent location. --------- , it is within walking distance of schools and a **18.** major shopping center. --------- So, it is hoped that this increased supply **19.** will help provide more affordable housing. Some local residents have voiced concern that the increased population will lead to crowding and traffic jams. The city council has announced plans to --------- roads in the **20.** area and provide more amenities such as sporting facilities and parks.

---

17. (A) effort
(B) price
(C) condition
(D) rate

18. (A) Indeed
(B) Nevertheless
(C) Similarly
(D) Therefore

19. (A) Sales of homes here have always been slow.
(B) Blair Valley is too far from Bradford for people to commute.
(C) House prices have been increasing rapidly in the last few years.
(D) Fortunately, the area is already well prepared for the additional residents.

20. (A) wide
(B) widen
(C) widely
(D) width

- [ ] latest　最新の
- [ ] housing development 住宅開発
- [ ] property　不動産（住宅）
- [ ] developer　開発業者
- [ ] within walking distance　徒歩圏内
- [ ] affordable　手頃な
- [ ] voice concern　懸念を示す
- [ ] city council　市議会
- [ ] amenity　施設

☑ **TIPS-17**

「句」で捉える！
⇒フレーズ [at a surprisng （　）]

☑ **TIPS-18**

ロジックを見る！
⇒空所の後は、「いい土地」の具体化

☑ **TIPS-19**

展開をつかむ！
⇒文選択問題。空所の後は、「住宅」の文脈

- [ ] commute　通勤する
- [ ] house price　住宅価格
- [ ] resident　住人

☑ **TIPS-20**

不定詞がポイント！
⇒[to＋（　）＋roads] を見て、動詞を選ぶ

Choose the best answer for each question.

Questions 21-24 refer to the following online chat discussion.

Greg Cole [3:28 P.M.]:
According to the lease agreement, we have to return the old office to its original condition when we move out. Who can lend a hand with the cleaning?

Seth Morris [3:29 P.M.]:
I thought we'd just hire a cleaning company to take care of that for us.

Greg Cole [3:31 P.M.]:
That's what I thought, too. Head office has asked us to do it ourselves as a part of the cost-cutting measures. It's not the busy season so I thought it was reasonable.

Amanda Andretti [3:33 P.M.]:
I've already made plans for the weekend. I don't mind lending a hand, but can it wait until next week?

Greg Cole [3:35 P.M.]:
I was planning on starting the cleaning work on Monday, so that's no problem.

Amanda Andretti [3:35 P.M.]:
What kind of work will we have to do?

Greg Cole [3:37 P.M.]:
We installed some shelves in the storage room to hold all of our cameras and lighting equipment. We need to get rid of all of them.

Seth Morris [3:45 P.M.]:
I suppose that means we need to remove the video editing booths and the brackets we installed for lighting.

Greg Cole [3:46 P.M.]:
That's right, Seth. I'll supply all the tools, and we'll rent a truck to carry away all the materials.

Greg Cole [3:49 P.M.]:
If any of you are too busy with your current projects, let me know.

☐ lease agreement
　賃貸契約書
☐ lend a hand　手を貸す
☐ reasonable　妥当な
☐ install
　～を備え付ける
☐ carry away
　～を運び出す

21. What are the writers mostly discussing?

(A) Complying with a rental agreement
(B) Finding a new location for their office
(C) Making a trip to company headquarters
(D) Delivering a presentation to a client

22. At 3:33 P.M., what does Ms. Andretti mean when she writes, "I've already made plans for the weekend"?

(A) She has prepared for a project.
(B) She cannot attend a celebration.
(C) She is in charge of an event.
(D) She would like to work at another time.

23. What kind of business do the writers most likely work for?

(A) A storage facility
(B) A production company
(C) A cleaning company
(D) A conference center

24. According to the online chat discussion, why might someone contact Mr. Cole?

(A) A piece of equipment is missing.
(B) A floor plan is not suitable.
(C) A deadline is approaching.
(D) A suitable candidate has been found.

☑ **TIPS-21**

最初のセリフに注目！
⇒本文のlease agreementをキャッチしよう

☐ comply with ～に従う
☐ headquarter 本社
☐ deliver a presentation プレゼンする

☑ **TIPS-22**

ターゲット文(" ")の後にヒント！
⇒「来週まで待って」のニュアンスを読む

☐ attend ～に参加する
☐ be in charge of ～の担当である

☑ **TIPS-23**

「業種」を推測する！
⇒video editing boothsなどの語句から探る

☐ storage 保管、倉庫

☑ **TIPS-24**

指示を見抜く！
⇒Cole氏のlet me knowがヒント

☐ equipment 装備
☐ suitable 適切である
☐ deadline 締切
☐ candidate 候補者

【意図問題】（Part4）設問のターゲット文（"　　　"）の意味を問う問題です。
これは前後を流れが分からないと解けない文脈問題でもあります。難問の確率が
高いので要注意！

part**1**　 22

Look at the picture and choose the statement that best describes what
you see.

1. (A) (B) (C) (D)

2.(A) (B) (C) (D)

> ☑ **TIPS-1**
>
> 「顔」の向きが出る！
> ⇒人の視線や車の方向に
> 　注目
>
> □ face　顔を向ける
> □ be lined up　並ぶ
> □ move　〜を運ぶ
> □ lift　〜を持ち上げる

> ☑ **TIPS-2**
>
> 共通点を見つける！
> ⇒人物（複数）写真では、
> 　動作・状態の共通点を
> 　探すのがセオリー
>
> □ hang　〜をつるす
> □ pass out　〜を配る
> □ refreshment　軽食
> □ put on　〜を着る
> □ beverage　飲み物
> □ venue　場所

Choose the best response to each question or statement.

3. (A) (B) (C)

4. (A) (B) (C)

5. (A) (B) (C)

part**3** 24

Listen to a short conversation, and choose the best answer to each question.

6. What change are the speakers discussing?

(A) An updated vacation policy
(B) A new staff member
(C) Some building renovations
(D) Some new transportation options

7. What does the man say will happen as a result of the change?

(A) Some shipping delays will be avoided.
(B) An employee handbook will be revised.
(C) Some furniture will be ordered.
(D) The office will open earlier.

8. What will happen at the company next month?

(A) A promotional campaign will be launched.
(B) A contract will be finalized.
(C) Devices will be distributed.
(D) Important clients will visit.

☑ TIPS

「依頼文」をマスター！
⇒Will you?などの依頼
　文は定番。確実に得点
　しよう

☑ TIPS-6

ルールの変更が出る！
⇒出張や休暇などの社内
　ルール変更は定番

☐ policy　方針
☐ renovation　改装
☐ transportation　交通

☑ TIPS-7

主張を聞く！
⇒we'll have to〜が耳
　印。直後がヒント

☐ shipping delay　出荷
　の遅れ
☐ revise　〜を改訂する

☑ TIPS-8

next monthがキーワー
ド！
⇒キーワードを含む文
　がヒント

☐ promotional
　campaign　宣伝キャ
　ンペーン
☐ launch　〜を開始する
☐ finalize　〜を終了さ
　せる

Listen to a short talk, and choose the best answer to each question.

9. Where do the listeners most likely work?

(A) At a shoe store
(B) At a television station
(C) At a sporting venue
(D) At an advertising agency

10. What does the speaker imply when he says, "They're really something"?

(A) He thinks a price is too high.
(B) He is impressed with a performance.
(C) He cannot remember the name of a team.
(D) He would like to end a relationship.

11. What does the speaker hope to schedule in May?

(A) A meeting with a client
(B) A press release
(C) A product launch
(D) A photo session

☑ **TIPS-9**

「職種」をイメージ！
⇒冒頭のワードから、ど
んな仕事かを推測する

☐ television station
テレビ局
☐ venue　会場
☐ advertising agency
広告代理店

☑ **TIPS-10**

直後を聞く！
⇒ターゲット文の後、
playing extremely
wellがヒント

☐ be impressed　感動
する
☐ relationship　関係

☑ **TIPS-11**

Mayが耳印！
⇒キーワードMayを含む
文、I'd like to〜がヒ
ント

Choose the best answer to complete the sentence.

12. Many of the ------- customers at Harold's Café stopped coming after the new menu was introduced.

(A) regular
(B) regularly
(C) regularity
(D) regulate

13. Divine Airlines gives passengers the ------- to decline meal services for a reduced ticket price.

(A) optional
(B) option
(C) optionally
(D) opted

14. Although Glendale Appliances have an excellent customer ------- score, their sales have been lower than expected.

(A) satisfactory
(B) satisfy
(C) satisfied
(D) satisfaction

15. As demand for swimwear is low during the winter months, the factory has ramped down -------.

(A) productive
(B) production
(C) productively
(D) produce

16. EMT Enterprises has hired a consultant to find an ------- way to reduce production costs without affecting quality.

(A) effect
(B) effectively
(C) effective
(D) effectiveness

☑ **TIPS-12**

選択肢の品詞がバラバラ！
⇒品詞問題。[the+（ ）
　+名詞]

☑ **TIPS-13**

theの後は「名詞」！
⇒品詞問題。[give+O
　+O]のパターン

□ passenger　乗客
□ decline　～を断る
□ reduced price　割
　価格

☑ **TIPS-14**

「名詞＋名詞」のフレー
ズ！
⇒例えば、reception
　desk（受付カウンター）
　など

☑ **TIPS-15**

消去法で解く！
⇒二つの名詞、
　productionとproduce
　の違いは？

□ ramp down　徐々
　下がる
□ production　生産(量
□ produce　農産物

☑ **TIPS-16**

空所の後の品詞を
チェック！
⇒品詞問題。[an+（ ）
　+way]

□ production cost
　産コスト
□ affect　～に影響を
　える

Choose the best answer to complete the text.
Questions 17-20 refer to the following memo.

To: All staff
From: Rentaro Hamada
Subject: Sunset Rider
Date: May 21

As I am sure you are aware, Hanson Farms --------- the production
                                          17.
company involved with *Sunset Rider* to use our southernmost fields
as a filming location. The film is --------- in theaters, and to show their
                                   18.
appreciation, the production company has set up an arrangement with
the GHT Cinemas whereby Hanson Farms' employees can get free
admission. Simply show your employee identification badge to the staff
at the box office and you should receive a free --------- Unfortunately, the
                                                19.
offer does not extend to friends and family members. ---------
                                                      20.

Sincerely,
Rentaro Hamada

---

17. (A) allows
    (B) is allowing
    (C) was allowed
    (D) allowed

18. (A) finally
    (B) final
    (C) finalize
    (D) finality

19. (A) souvenir
    (B) beverage
    (C) ticket
    (D) snack

20. (A) So, you can bring up to three additional people at no extra cost.
    (B) If you take them along, it will be necessary to buy tickets.
    (C) We hope they will allow us to use the land again.
    (D) Please mention this to customers when you take reservations.

□ production company
  制作会社
□ southernmost 最南
  端の
□ appreciation 感謝
□ set up an
  arrangement 取り決
  めをする
□ free admission
  入場料無料
□ identification badge
  ID バッジ
□ box office チケット
  売場
□ extend
  〜に拡大する

☑ **TIPS-17**

allowの語法は？
⇒語法は速攻で解こう。
  [allow＋O＋to do]

☑ **TIPS-18**

文構造を確認！
⇒be動詞の後には何が
  来る？

☑ **TIPS-19**

言い換えから連想しよ
う！
⇒直前のfree admission
  がヒント

☑ **TIPS-20**

文脈をプラス／マイナ
スで見る！
⇒文選択問題
  Unfortunately以下
  は、マイナス（チケッ
  ト有料）の文脈

□ additional 追加の
□ at no extra cost
  追加料金なしで
□ take reservations
  予約する

Choose the best answer for each question.
Questions 21-24 refer to the following article.

Glengarry's Growth Gets a Boost

By Randy Heinlein, June 23

Glengarry has been experiencing steady growth in recent years, and the addition of a music festival to its yearly events calendar has suddenly made it an attractive destination for international guests. These two factors have resulted in it meeting the state's requirements for an international airport. This week, permission was granted to start construction of an international terminal alongside the city's current domestic terminal. Bidding for the project will begin this week with the understanding construction must be completed by April next year. This will be necessary to ensure international visitors to the Glengarry Music Festival can take advantage of the new transportation routes.

Spokesperson for the project, Alison McCann has announced that the airport authority will start hiring staff a couple of months ahead of the opening in order to provide the required training. There will also be work for immigration officials and security personnel. In addition to jobs working for the Airport Authority itself, people will be employed by the airlines as ground crew and aircraft maintenance staff. She anticipates that more than 200 additional people will be employed by businesses within the terminal. These include restaurants and specialty stores.

21. According to the article, what will soon be available for Glengarry residents?

(A) An expanded airport
(B) A new concert venue
(C) A visitors' center
(D) A new college

22. What event will be held in April?

(A) A scientific conference
(B) A music festival
(C) A company launch
(D) A sporting competition

23. What employment opportunity is NOT mentioned in the article?

(A) Security workers
(B) Mechanical engineers
(C) Tour guides
(D) Store clerks

24. In the article, the word "opening" in paragraph 2, line 3 is closest in meaning to

(A) vacancy
(B) inauguration
(C) outlet
(D) availability

☑ **TIPS-23**

選択肢のワードをサーチ!
⇒NOT問題。言い換えに注意しながら、対応箇所を見つける

☐ employment opportunity　雇用機会
☐ store clerk　店員

☑ **TIPS-24**

消去法で対応！
⇒語句問題。意味の分かる選択肢からチェック

CHAPTER
7

【写真問題】（Part1）　人物写真は「動作」、風景写真は「目立つもの」が問われ
るのが基本です。ですが、近年はどちらでもない日常風景も出ます。リスニング
力を高めましょう。

part**1**　 26

Look at the picture and choose the statement that best describes what
you see.

1. (A) (B) (C) (D)

TIPS-1

人物の違いも出る！
⇒動作・状態の細部に注
　意

☐ rest A on B　Aを
　に置く
☐ put on glasses
　眼鏡をかける
☐ lap　膝
☐ overhead rack　頭
　の棚

2.(A) (B) (C) (D)

TIPS-2

目立つ人物をチェック！
⇒セオリー通り、動作を
　聞こう

☐ step out of
　〜から降りる
☐ paved path　舗装
　れた道

part2 27

Choose the best response to each question or statement.

3. (A) (B) (C)

4. (A) (B) (C)

5. (A) (B) (C)

☑ TIPS

トリッキーな応答に注意！
⇒A or Bの選択疑問文では、素直じゃない応答が出る

☐ make up one's mind
　決定する
☐ charge　〜を請求する
☐ daily special　日替わり

part3 28

Listen to a short conversation, and choose the best answer to each question.

6. What does the man want to discuss with the woman?

(A) A business trip
(B) A building design
(C) A product function
(D) A news program

☑ TIPS-6

会話トピックは冒頭！
⇒最初のセリフに集中しよう

☐ function　機能

7. What does the woman say she will do after lunch?

(A) Attend a conference
(B) Visit a construction site
(C) Watch a video
(D) Hire a consultant

☑ TIPS-7

設問will doをチェック！
⇒「これから」に関する箇所がヒント

8. Why does the man recommend a different mode of transport?

(A) A train service has been canceled.
(B) He would like to call the woman.
(C) There are some traffic jams.
(D) The car is being repaired.

☑ TIPS-8

「渋滞」が出る！
⇒交通トピックの定番

☐ transport　交通機関
☐ traffic jam　交通渋滞

Listen to a short talk, and choose the best answer to each question.

9. What will take place next?

(A) A film screening
(B) A news broadcast
(C) A recital
(D) A seminar

10. Who is probably scheduled to speak?

(A) A musician
(B) An editor
(C) A career advisor
(D) A film producer

11. What are audience members encouraged to do?

(A) Purchase tickets
(B) Attend a reception
(C) Read a schedule
(D) Ask questions

Choose the best answer to complete the sentence.

12. Construction of the new warehouse will begin on June 19 ------- on the weather.

(A) depending
(B) depended
(C) dependable
(D) dependability

☑ TIPS-12

分詞構文は＋α！
⇒S＋V（主従）関係を考
　えよう

13. The factory is operating at a ------- production level until sales pick up in summer.

(A) reducing
(B) reduced
(C) reduction
(D) reduce

☑ TIPS-13

SV関係に注目！
⇒～ing or～ed
　[production level is
　（　）]

□ operate　稼働する
□ pick up　回復する

14. Only ------- members of the Haliburton Country Club are allowed to enter the grounds unless special permission has been granted.

(A) verifying
(B) verification
(C) verify
(D) verified

☑ TIPS-14

受け身が大事！
⇒～ing or ～ed
　[members are（　）]

□ verify ～を承認する
□ be allowed to do　～
　するのが許される
□ permission　許可
□ grant　～を与える

15. A highly ------- lawyer from Barnes and Hope Solicitors will give the keynote address at this year's Hampton Legal Conference.

(A) respecting
(B) respected
(C) respective
(D) respect

☑ TIPS-15

空所周辺だけで解く！
⇒～ing or ～ed
　[lawyer is（　）]

□ keynote address
　貴重講演

16. A memo ------- use of company vehicles for private errands was sent to every employee.

(A) concerned
(B) concerns
(C) concerning
(D) concern

☑ TIPS-16

ひっかけに注意！
⇒[A memo is（　）
　use of ～]

□ concern
　～に関係している
□ company vehicle
　社用車
□ errand　用事

Choose the best answer to complete the text.
Questions 17-20 refer to the following article.

According to *Atlantic Trader* research, startup companies that hire consultants have a far higher success rate than those that do not. --------- **17.** However, the reasons behind the tendency need to be explored. Hiring a consultant is not cheap so it -------- **18.** to reason that only startups with a lot of capital or wealthy investors will have the opportunity to use one. ----------, **19.** consultants like to be associated with successful businesses, so only businesses which appear to have a lot of potential from the outset can attract competent consultants. The Canadian government has recently taken these ---------- **20.** into consideration. It is now offering consultancy services to startups which are not on such secure financial footing from the outset.

17. (A) As a result, there are fewer and fewer consultants available.
    (B) Wealthy investors rarely need such expert advice.
    (C) The government is unwilling to address the issue in any way.
    (D) This seems to suggest that all startup businesses should hire consultants.

18. (A) stands
    (B) denies
    (C) applies
    (D) resorts

19. (A) And so
    (B) Nevertheless
    (C) Furthermore
    (D) Accordingly

20. (A) revisions
    (B) observations
    (C) acquisitions
    (D) ultimatums

□ startup company
　ベンチャー企業
□ tendency　傾向
□ explore　～を探る
□ wealthy investor
　裕福な投資家
□ be associated with
　～に関わる
□ from the outset　最初から
□ competent　有能な
□ take into consideration
　～を考慮する
□ consultancy service
　コンサルトサービス
□ financial footing
　財政基盤

✓ TIPS-17

文脈をつかむ！
⇒文選択問題。コンサルタントを肯定する文脈

□ rarely
　めったに～ない
□ be unwilling to do
　～したがらない
□ address the issue
　問題に取り組む

✓ TIPS-18

知らない場合はスルー！
⇒イディオム[(　) to reason]

✓ TIPS-19

＋αの記号！
⇒空所後は「追加」情報

✓ TIPS-20

ハイレベルにトライ！
⇒「語彙＋文脈」で解く

Choose the best answer for each question.
Questions 21-24 refer to the following e-mail.

To:	Bob Davies <bdavies@stratonhs.com>
From:	Glenda Rogers <grogrs@novabird.com>
Subject:	10 Mardella Drive
Date:	September 19

Dear Mr. Davies,

I tried using the Stratton Home Services new mobile application for the first time this morning and, unfortunately, it does not seem to be working correctly. I input the details of the work I needed to have carried out several times and hit the "submit" button, but I did not receive a confirmation message.

I am not sure whether the application has taken my work order without sending a confirmation or whether the work order itself was lost. If the order has been recorded, you may find three copies of it. I hope that I will not be charged multiple times for the work.

In case the work order has not been received, please allow me to make my request by e-mail as I have done in the past for various plumbing and cleaning services. I have received a notice from the Mermaid Waters City Council, which notifies residents that inspections of their gardens will be carried out to ensure that there are no plant species that damage the environment. If such species are found, landowners will have to pay an expensive fine. I do not have time to do the work myself as I am leaving on an extended business trip from tomorrow evening.

I will be available for you to come around and give a price estimate tomorrow morning. I will give you the key to the back garden at that time so that your employees can carry out the work in my absence.

Sincerely,
Glenda Rogers

□ confirmation 確認
□ record ～を記憶する
□ multiple times 複数回
□ make one's request 要求する
□ plumbing 配管
□ carry out ～を実行する
□ plant species 植物種
□ landowner 所有者
□ fine 罰金
□ estimate 見積り

21. What is the purpose of the e-mail?
(A) To inquire about a work request
(B) To notify a client of a new service
(C) To offer assistance with a project
(D) To provide advice to a local resident

22. What is mentioned about Ms. Rogers garden?
(A) It has received an award.
(B) It is regularly maintained by Stratton Home Services.
(C) It will be inspected by a city official.
(D) It is visible from the street.

23. What is NOT implied about Ms. Rogers?
(A) She has used Stratton Home Services before.
(B) She will ask the council to reschedule her inspection.
(C) She owns the property at 10 Mardella Drive.
(D) She will take a business trip soon.

24. When is Ms. Rogers available to meet an employee of Stratton Home Services?
(A) This morning
(B) This evening
(C) Tomorrow morning
(D) Tomorrow evening

☑ **TIPS-22**

gardenをサーチ！
⇒「庭」への言及は第3段落

☐ receive an award
　受賞する
☐ regularly　定期的に
☐ inspect
　〜を検査する

☑ **TIPS-23**

選択肢との対応箇所を
速読！
⇒NOT問題。第3段落に
　ヒント

☐ council　議会
☐ reschedule
　スケジュールを変更する
☐ property　土地
☐ business trip　出張

☑ **TIPS-24**

「時」をサーチ！
⇒今後の予定は、文末で
　言及される

【応答問題】（Part2）　疑問詞アリの Q に対して、Yes/No で応答するシンプルな問題は減少傾向です。ふつうの文（平叙文）の Q に対して、疑問文で応答する問題など、応用力が大事！

part 1　 30

Look at the picture and choose the statement that best describes what you see.

1. (A) (B) (C) (D)

2. (A) (B) (C) (D)

☑ TIPS-1

人物の有無を意識して！
⇒消去法で正解率アップ

□ stack
　〜を積み重ねる
□ courtyard　中庭
□ diner　食事客

☑ TIPS-2

風景写真のbeingは不正解！
⇒受け身の進行形が出る

□ stroll　〜をぶらつく
□ arched　アーチ型の
□ light fitting　照明器具
□ suspend　〜を吊す
□ polisher　床磨き機

Choose the best response to each question or statement.

3. (A) (B) (C)

4. (A) (B) (C)

5. (A) (B) (C)

Listen to a short conversation, and choose the best answer to each question.

6. Where do the speakers most likely work?

(A) At a car dealership
(B) At a newsagent
(C) At a magazine publisher
(D) At a museum

7. What problem is being discussed?

(A) An event was canceled.
(B) Some visitors have been delayed.
(C) A brochure is not ready.
(D) Some exhibits are not ready.

8. What will the man most likely do next?

(A) Read a manual
(B) Print some invitations
(C) Fill out a form
(D) Contact a photographer

☑ TIPS

疑問文の応答に慣れよう！
⇒[Q:平叙文→A:疑問文]
　のパターン

☐ reception　受付
☐ historical attraction
　歴史的名所

☑ TIPS-6

「業種」をタテ読み！
⇒選択肢を先読みして、
　放送を聞こう

☑ TIPS-7

トラブルをキャッチ！
⇒What problem〜？は
　定番

☐ be delayed
　遅延する
☐ brochure
　パンフレット
☐ exhibit　展示

☑ TIPS-8

do next問題！
⇒「次の展開」は、文末の
　I'll〜にヒント

☐ invitation　招待状
☐ fill out　〜に記入する

Listen to a short talk, and choose the best answer to each question.

9. What will happen this weekend?

(A) Computers will be upgraded.
(B) Some furniture will be delivered.
(C) Offices will be painted.
(D) An event will be held.

10. What are listeners asked to do?

(A) Take home personal items
(B) Come to an event venue
(C) Wear appropriate clothing
(D) Read an employee manual

11. When will the planned work be completed?

(A) By Monday
(B) By Tuesday
(C) By Thursday
(D) By Friday

✅ **TIPS-9**

トピックは冒頭！
⇒What will happen
〜？は「出来事」を問う
定番

☐ deliver 〜を届ける

✅ **TIPS-10**

「お願い」をキャッチ！
⇒Please〜以外のお願
い表現も出る

☐ personal item 私物
☐ venue 場所
☐ appropriate 相応し
い

✅ **TIPS-11**

作業の完了！
⇒「曜日」を耳印にしよう

Choose the best answer to complete the sentence.

12. Because Hal Whitman's online videos have such a large online -------, he has made a lot of money through advertising revenue.

(A) following
(B) followed
(C) to follow
(D) follows

☑ **TIPS-12**

空所の品詞を見抜け！
⇒[a large online
 (   )]をカタマリで捉える

13. Mr. Holland's efforts have paid off for the company in many ways, earning him the ------- of his colleagues.

(A) respectability
(B) respect
(C) respecting
(D) respected

☑ **TIPS-13**

2つの名詞を攻略！
⇒意味の違いが出る

☐ pay off　うまくいく
☐ colleague　同僚

14. The new recruits expressed interest in ------- the manufacturing process first hand.

(A) observation
(B) observer
(C) observational
(D) observing

☑ **TIPS-14**

空所の後がポイント！
⇒[in+ (   )+N]

☐ recruit　新入社員
☐ express interest
　関心を示す
☐ manufacturing
　process　製造過程

15. ------- the participants and their families was a huge task for organizers of the National Amateur Sports Championships.

(A) Accommodation
(B) Accommodating
(C) Accommodate
(D) Accommodates

☑ **TIPS-15**

主語＝(動)名詞！

☐ participant　競技者
☐ huge task　大きな課題
☐ organizer　主催者

16. Hanson Engineering has returned to profitability under the excellent ------- of Clive Winger.

(A) directing
(B) directive
(C) direction
(D) direct

☑ **TIPS-16**

名詞のカタマリをつかむ！
⇒[the excellent+
 (   )]

☐ profitability　収益

Choose the best answer to complete the text.
Questions 17-20 refer to the following advertisement.

Vladimir Vaults offer businesses secure storage solutions for sensitive documents. We have storage for both --------- files and computer data
17.
in our state-of-the-art storage facilities. We even provide a conversion service which transfers physical files to data formats and permanently destroys the originals ensuring perfect --------- Our data centers in New
18.
York, California, Texas, and Illinois hold duplicate copies of all the files trusted to us. This --------- that in the unlikely event that a mishap occurs
19.
at one of our locations, no client will ever be inconvenienced. --------- Our
20.
centers are staffed 24 hours a day and your files will be made available the moment you complete the verification process.

☐ secure storage
　安全な保管
☐ sensitive document
　機密文書
☐ state-of-the-art
　最先端の
☐ conversion　変換
☐ data format　データ
　形式
☐ duplicate　複製の
☐ ensure
　～を保証する
☐ mishap　事故
☐ verification　確認

17. (A) physically
　　(B) physicality
　　(C) physicals
　　(D) physical

18. (A) confidentiality
　　(B) confidential
　　(C) confide
　　(D) confidentially

19. (A) requires
　　(B) considers
　　(C) ensures
　　(D) assumes

20. (A) Our file recovery process is completely automated.
　　(B) Clients can retrieve their files at any time of day.
　　(C) Files can take up to a week to retrieve from remote locations.
　　(D) At present, we cannot store files in more than one location.

Choose the best answer for each question.
Questions 21-24 refer to the following article.

The Stirling Bridge in Stirling has long been a favorite of tourists visiting Scotland. Since it was recognized as important historical landmark almost a hundred years ago, it has not been used for its intended function. Instead, it serves only as a landmark and a viewing platform for visitors to the area.

The person most familiar with the bridge is perhaps a man who has spent the greater part of his life ensuring its upkeep. Reginald Moss has been hired by the regional council to ensure the bridge is safe and free of weather damage since he was 26 years old. Mr. Moss believes that the visitors probably come for the magnificent views the bridge affords but states that the Bridge Restaurant is one of the areas most underrated attractions. He encourages all the travelers he meets to stay for lunch or dinner there. Indeed, the restaurant has an outstanding menu with many original dishes. It alone seems worth the trip.

If you are planning a trip through Scotland in August, the Stirling Bridge is something you should really consider adding to your itinerary. The Stirling Marching Band is providing free nightly performances at the base of the bridge all month. It is truly a magical experience and an attraction that is sure to attract more and more attention in the future.

21. What is suggested about Stirling Bridge?

(A) It no longer carries traffic.
(B) It was destroyed many years ago.
(C) It has won a design award.
(D) It charges a toll to drivers who cross it.

22. Who most likely is Mr. Moss?

(A) An architect
(B) A maintenance worker
(C) A tour guide
(D) A chef

23. What does Mr. Moss recommend visitors to Stirling Bridge do?

(A) Take photographs from the bridge
(B) Join a guided tour
(C) Dine at the restaurant
(D) Stay at a local hotel

Sidebar:
- historical landmark 歴史的ランドマーク
- viewing platform 展望台
- upkeep 維持
- regional council 地方議会
- underrated 過小価された
- outstanding 素晴しい
- itinerary 旅程

TIPS-21
キーワード・サーチ！
⇒Stirling Bridgeをサーチして、周辺を読む

- toll 通行料

TIPS-22
Who問題→職業！
⇒選択肢を先読みして、本文を見る

TIPS-23
オススメは何？
⇒Mr.Mossをサーチ。直後、彼が「見所」に言及する

- guided tour ガイドツアー
- dine 食事をする

24. What will happen in August?

(A) The bridge will be closed to visitors
(B) A special performance will be given.
(C) A celebrity guest will make an appearance.
(D) Discount tickets will be made available.

 TIPS-24

8月のイベントは？
⇒Augustをサーチ。周
辺を読めば即答

□ make an appearance
登場する
□ discount ticket 割
引チケット

【説明文と図表のクロス問題】（Part4） 説明文と図表をクロスさせて解く難問が出ます。設問、選択肢、図表を先読みしないと対応するのは至難の業。チャレンジ問題と考えましょう。

part 1 34

Look at the picture and choose the statement that best describes what you see.

1. (A) (B) (C) (D)

2. (A) (B) (C) (D)

Choose the best response to each question or statement.

3. (A) (B) (C)

4. (A) (B) (C)

5. (A) (B) (C)

☑ **TIPS**

Don't you ～?
= Do you～?
⇒「否定疑問文＝ふつう
　の疑問文」と考えよう

☐ head back　戻る
☐ banquet　宴会

part**3** 36

Listen to a short conversation, and choose the best answer to each question.

6. What are the speakers discussing?

(A) A computer program
(B) A corporate merger
(C) A department budget
(D) A sales target

☑ **TIPS-6**

トピックを攻略！
⇒セオリー通り、冒頭を
　聞こう

☐ budget　予算
☐ sales target　販売目
　標

7. What does the man mean when he says, "There's no debate"?

(A) Some changes must be reversed.
(B) The woman is certain to get a promotion.
(C) A survey was difficult to interpret.
(D) A new employee will be hired.

☑ **TIPS-7**

まちぶせリスニング！
⇒ターゲット文＝耳印

☐ reverse　～を元に戻
　す
☐ get a promotion　昇
　進する
☐ interpret　～を解釈
　する

8. What will happen on Friday?

(A) Some clients will make a visit.
(B) Some construction work will begin.
(C) A section meeting will be held.
(D) A staff member will retire from the company.

☑ **TIPS-8**

Friday＝耳印！
⇒これからの出来事は文
　末で言及

☐ make a visit　来訪す
　る

Listen to a short talk, and choose the best answer to each question.

Oil Change Rates (4 liters)	
Premium Plus	$70
Premium	$60
Standard	$50
Budget	$40

9. Who most likely is the caller?

(A) A mechanic
(B) A company president
(C) A salesperson
(D) A delivery driver

TIPS-9

電話の話し手は、会話冒頭でイメージ！

10. Look at the graphic. How much was the speaker charged for the work?

(A) $70
(B) $60
(C) $50
(D) $40

TIPS-10

図表を先読み！
⇒数字以外を先読みして、待ち伏せリスニング

11. What does the speaker intend to do on Monday?

(A) Process an order
(B) Take a vacation
(C) Switch to a new vehicle
(D) Request reimbursement

TIPS-11

言い換えに注意！
⇒Mondayが耳印。これからのことは、文末に集中

☐ process
　～を処理する
☐ reimbursement
　い戻し

Choose the best answer to complete the sentence.

12. Employees must notify ------- immediate supervisor if they intend to take time off work for any reason.

(A) their
(B) theirs
(C) themselves
(D) they

13. Ms. Granger said that she would make all of the arrangements for the year-end banquet -------.

(A) hers
(B) herself
(C) she
(D) her

14. None of the trainees know that ------- are expected to bring a change of clothes to the first training session.

(A) their
(B) theirs
(C) them
(D) they

15. Mr. Hargraves asked a number of other employees help ------- administer a survey to the seminar participants.

(A) himself
(B) him
(C) his
(D) he

16. Ms. Greene invited an engineer whom ------- met at a conference to apply for the department head position at her firm.

(A) herself
(B) hers
(C) she
(D) her

☑ **TIPS-12**

「格」を攻略！
⇒[(　) immediate supervisor]

☐ immediate supervisor 直属の上司
☐ take time off work 仕事を休む

☑ **TIPS-13**

「自分自身で」は？
⇒I must do it myself. の用法

☐ make arrangements 段取りをつける

☑ **TIPS-14**

主語＝「主格」！

☐ trainee　訓練生
☐ be expected to do ～することを期待する

☑ **TIPS-15**

Mr.Hargravesの「目的格」は？

☐ administer　～を行う
☐ survey　調査

☑ **TIPS-16**

whom以下の文構造を見る！
⇒[whom (　) met (at a conference)～]

☐ apply for ～に応募する

Choose the best answer to complete the text.
Questions 17-20 refer to the following e-mail.

To:	Ralph Wang <rwang@winstonem.com>
From:	Glenda Singh <gsingh@harbousidecc.org>
Date:	October 18
Subject:	Elevator inspections
Attachment:	addresses

Dear Mr. Wang,

Today, it has come to -------- attention that there are several elevators
17.
around town whose maintenance report has not been updated after

inspections. I would like to remind you that posting an updated

maintenance report in the elevator is part of the service Winston

Elevator Health and Safety has been hired to carry out. --------
18.

The council -------- for the inspections. Therefore, we assume that
19.
they have been carried out and we are permitting the use of the

elevators on October 19. Please visit the three addresses listed in the

attachment and provide the required paperwork -------- closing time
20.
tomorrow.

Sincerely,
Glenda Singh
Winston City Council

□ remind ～に気づか
る
□ post ～を公表する
□ attachment 添付
□ paperwork 事務書

TIPS-17

名詞を修飾する「格」
は？
⇒[( ) attention]

TIPS-18

reportとreport！
⇒文選択問題。前文との
ワード繋がりを見よ

□ stipulate ～ を 規
する
□ at one's convenien
都合のいいときに
□ alert ～に警告する
□ oversight 見落とし
□ extension （期間）
延長

17. (A) your
(B) his
(C) their
(D) my

18. (A) Local laws stipulate that elevators may not be used without a
report displayed.
(B) Please carry out the inspections at the affected businesses at your
earliest convenience.
(C) Thank you for alerting us to the oversight by our staff.
(D) Otherwise, your application for an extension may be denied.

19. (A) is charging
(B) charged
(C) has been charged
(D) will be charged

20. (A) on
(B) by
(C) since
(D) until

 TIPS-19

受け身が大事！
⇒「(現在も点検が)課されている」ニュアンス

 TIPS-20

「期限」ワード！
⇒「〜までに〜して下さい」は文末の定型

part 7

Choose the best answer for each question.
Questions 21-24 refer to the following e-mail.

To:	Udom Mugadu <umugadu@bluenova.com>
From:	Sally Curuthers <scuruthers@jewelpc.com>
Date:	28 November
Subject:	Writing

Dear Mr. Mugadu,

Jewel Publishing Company (JPC) is interested in publishing a book on classic car restoration, and I am looking for writers to contribute to the contents. Although JPC is based in London, we are well aware of your fame in restoration circles having seen your weekly television program on Channel 13. We are also aware how busy the show's production schedule must keep you.

In return for your allowing us to credit you as one of the book's writers, we would like to offer you a generous royalty. Furthermore, we would hire an assistant writer to do most of the writing work for you so that you only have to spend minimal time on the project.

Please let me know if you would like to be attached to the project. I will be happy to fly to Manchester to meet with you at your agent's offices there. I have already been in touch with Ms. White, who was kind enough to give me this e-mail address so that I may contact you directly. I would be happy to arrange a meeting at a time that suits you in the next two weeks. Please let us know if you are not interested as we are considering other celebrities for the work.

Sincerely,
Sally Caruthers
JPC

☐ restoration 復元
☐ contribute to
　〜に寄与する
☐ be aware of
　〜に気づく
☐ generous 寛大な
☐ royalty 印税
☐ be in touch with
　〜と連絡を取る

21. Who most likely is Ms. Caruthers?

(A) An editor
(B) A photographer
(C) A mechanic
(D) A producer

22. What is implied about Mr. Mugadu?

(A) He has helped write several books.
(B) He is a well-known personality.
(C) He likes to travel.
(D) He entered a competition.

23. How will JPC help Mr. Mugadu?

(A) By providing a transportation allowance
(B) By assigning him a private office
(C) By employing an assistant
(D) By extending his deadline

24. What is Mr. Mugadu encouraged to do?

(A) Hire a new talent agent
(B) Meet with Ms. Caruthers
(C) Take a trip to London
(D) Introduce a celebrity

TIPS-21

メールの送り手は？
⇒Who問題。職業／職種
をつかもう

TIPS-22

メールの受け手は？
⇒冒頭から情報を集める

☐ personality　有名人
☐ competition　競争

TIPS-23

メリットをサーチ！
⇒JPCによる提案は、
We would〜で提示

☐ allowance　手当
☐ extend　〜を延長する
☐ deadline　締切

TIPS-24

要望のパターン！
⇒Please〜やI' d like to
〜などがヒント

☐ celebrity　有名人

CHAPTER
10

【文法 & 品詞問題】（Part5） TOEIC テストで最も点数が取りやすいのが「文法 & 品詞問題」です。ミスを最小限にして、確実に得点しましょう。特に「品詞問題」はノーミス必須！

part 1 38

Look at the picture and choose the statement that best describes what you see.

1. (A) (B) (C) (D)

2. (A) (B) (C) (D)

☑ **TIPS-1**

目立つアクションを見る！
⇒動作チェックは基本

☐ a basket of
　ひとかごの
☐ shade　日陰
☐ sweep　～を掃く
☐ sidewalk　歩道

☑ **TIPS-2**

写真にないものは×！

☐ on each side of　～
　の両側に
☐ be lined up　並ぶ
☐ head down　～を通っ
　て進む
☐ a flight of stairs
　階段
☐ streetlight　街灯
☐ illuminate
　～を照らす
☐ storefront　店頭

Choose the best response to each question or statement.

3. (A) (B) (C)

4. (A) (B) (C)

5. (A) (B) (C)

part**3** 40

Listen to a short conversation, and choose the best answer to each question.

6. Why will the woman visit London next week?

(A) To take part in a tour
(B) To meet with a prospective client
(C) To interview some job applicants
(D) To purchase some equipment

7. What does the man suggest?

(A) Attending a theater production
(B) Visiting a museum
(C) Taking a train
(D) Having a meal together

8. What does the man offer the woman?

(A) Tickets to an event
(B) A set of product samples
(C) Some notes from a meeting
(D) An introduction to an acquaintance

Listen to a short talk, and choose the best answer to each question.

Col's Pizzeria–Coupon
Sunday
Any pasta dish with free entrée
Monday through Thursday
Any pizza with free desert
Friday
Any pizza with a free drink
Saturday
Any pasta dish with a free salad

---

9. What is mentioned about Col's Pizzeria?

(A) It has moved to a new location.
(B) It is under new management.
(C) It still uses its original menu.
(D) It has been operating for a long time.

> **☑ TIPS-9**
>
> 店の情報は冒頭！
> ⇒キーワード Col's
> Pizzeria直後にヒント

10. Where can listeners get the coupon?

(A) In the mail
(B) From a newspaper
(C) At a supermarket
(D) From a mobile application

> **☑ TIPS-10**
>
> 選択肢をタテ読み！
> ⇒選択肢をざっと見て、
> クーポン情報を予測

11. Look at the graphic. What can people who use the coupon today get for free?

(A) An entrée
(B) A dessert
(C) A drink
(D) A salad

> **☑ TIPS-11**
>
> 「曜日」がポイント！
> ⇒まずは本文から、
> todayの情報をつかむ

Choose the best answer to complete the sentence.

12. Bison Corporation's return to ------- is a result of its increased focus on product quality.

(A) profitability
(B) profitable
(C) profited
(D) profitably

☑ TIPS-12

選択肢の品詞がバラバラ！
⇒品詞問題。主部の範囲を見抜こう

□ return　回復
□ product quality
　製品の品質

13. The Connor Valley has enjoyed ------- over the years due to its strong dairy industry.

(A) prosper
(B) prosperity
(C) prosperous
(D) prosperously

☑ TIPS-13

品詞問題は即答！

□ enjoy　〜を享受する
□ dairy　酪農

14. Survey results showed that most customers found Hammond Footwear -------, but not exceptional.

(A) satisfactorily
(B) satisfaction
(C) satisfy
(D) satisfactory

☑ TIPS-14

findの語法！
⇒品詞問題。[find+O+C]

□ survey result　調査結果
□ exceptional　特別な

15. *Mountain Hijinks* was praised for its ------- by judges at the Dawson Movie Festival.

(A) original
(B) originality
(C) origin
(D) originally

☑ TIPS-15

名詞が3つ！
⇒ (A)(B)(C)は名詞の可能性アリ

□ praise　〜を称賛する
□ judge　審査員

16. Ms. Cho gave an ------- presentation on the history of Hill Valley at the town visitors' bureau.

(A) information
(B) informatively
(C) informative
(D) inform

☑ TIPS-16

名詞を修飾するのは？
⇒品詞問題。[an (　　) presentation]

□ visitors' bureau
　観光局

Choose the best answer to complete the text.
Questions 17-20 refer to the following instructions.

The Oregon Bookshelf Assembly Instructions

The Oregon Bookshelf from Jax Furnishings is delivered to customers in pieces to reduce its size and save you money on shipping. It also makes it --------- to move furniture items into and out of your home. Inside the **17.** box, you will find all the screws and fasteners you will require for the --------- **18.** --------- Before you begin putting the unit together, please check the list of **19.** items on the back of these instructions against the contents of the box to make sure that there are no missing parts. --------- there are any missing **20.** items, please call our customer support line on 934-555-8348.

□ deliver ～を届ける
□ in pieces 細かく
□ screw ネジ
□ fastener 留め具
□ put ～ together
　組み立てる
□ instructions 説明書
□ missing parts 不足
　している部品

17. (A) cheaper
(B) lighter
(C) cozier
(D) easier

☑ TIPS-17

[make+(it/O)+C]か
ら意味を取る！
⇒ it = to move～

18. (A) assembly
(B) repairs
(C) packing
(D) extension

☑ TIPS-18

ネジは何に使う？
⇒「本棚の組み立て」と
　いう文脈を意識して

19. (A) You must come to our factory and pick up the item in person.
(B) Customer service inquiries are all handled online through our Web site.
(C) There is also a handy disposable screwdriver.
(D) Please do not attempt to construct the item yourself.

☑ TIPS-19

「ネジ→ドライバー」の
繋がり！
⇒文選択問題。前後の文
　脈を見る

□ in person 自分で
□ disposable 使い捨
　ての

20. (A) Because
(B) If
(C) Unless
(D) Although

☑ TIPS-20

定型文は即答！
⇒「もし～ならば、
　～にご連絡下さい」

Choose the best answer for each question.
Questions 21-24 refer to the following book review.

Before writing his account of the life of billionaire Kym Brandon, Stan Holmes was an award-winning journalist. His years covering business news for the *Financial Gazette* put him in an excellent position to understand the struggles Mr. Brandon had on his way to the top.

It is an exciting read, which is a hard feat to pull off considering that we all know how Mr. Brandon's life turned out in the end. One criticism many people have made of the book is that it is not balanced enough. Of course, Mr. Brandon is an excellent business person. Nevertheless, there has been some controversy along the way and very little of that is mentioned in this book. This may be part of an agreement the writer struck with Mr. Brandon in order to obtain his cooperation with the project. To be fair, the version I read in October was a preview copy and rumor has it, an extra chapter has been added to the version of the book that will be released in bookstores in December. Perhaps that will contain a little more about Mr. Brandon's less successful moments.

In writing the book, Mr. Holmes spent hundreds of hours with Mr. Brandon. From May to June this year, he traveled alongside Mr. Brandon to his various homes and golf clubs around the world. The access he was given to the famous billionaire gave Mr. Holmes an understanding of his personality that few others can claim.

To celebrate the book's release, Mr. Holmes will go on a book signing tour around the country. The dates and locations of the tour are available on the publisher's Web site.

21. What kind of book is being reviewed?
(A) A biography
(B) A travel guide
(C) A reference book
(D) A textbook

22. What criticism does the review mention?
(A) The book is a little too long.
(B) The information in the book is already out of date.
(C) The book only covers positive topics.
(D) The publisher did not print enough copies of the book.

□ billionaire 億万長者
□ award-winning 受賞歴のある
□ cover ～を取り扱う
□ struggle 苦闘、努力
□ feat 偉業
□ controversy 論争
□ personality 性格、個性

☑ **TIPS-21**

本のジャンルは冒頭！
⇒選択肢を先読みすれば、即答も可

☑ **TIPS-22**

批判のポイントは？
⇒否定語に注目する

□ out of date 時代おくれ
□ positive 肯定的な
□ publisher 出版社
□ enough copies 十分な部数

23. When does the book go on sale?

(A) In May
(B) In June
(C) In October
(D) In December

24. What is NOT indicated about Mr. Holmes?

(A) He has worked as a journalist.
(B) He has agreed to write a follow-up book.
(C) He has met Mr. Brandon in person.
(D) He will go on a book signing tour.

 TIPS-23

「月」をサーチ！
⇒複数の月に惑わされな
　いように

 TIPS-24

NOT問題は慎重に！
⇒選択肢と本文の比較検
　討

☐ follow-up　追跡

part**1** 42

Look at the picture and choose the statement that best describes what you see.

1. (A) (B) (C) (D)

2.(A) (B) (C) (D)

✓ **TIPS-1**

動詞キャッチが基本!

☐ pass through
　通り抜ける
☐ vehicle　乗り物

✓ **TIPS-2**

写真の共通点を見る!

☐ undergo　〜を受け
☐ head　〜に向かう
☐ handrail　手すり
☐ pass　〜を手渡す

Choose the best response to each question or statement.

3. (A) (B) (C)

4. (A) (B) (C)

5. (A) (B) (C)

part**3** 44

Henderson Event Space

4th Floor	Roof Deck	
3rd Floor	McPherson Room	
2nd Floor	Kinsen Room	Weldon Room
1st Floor	Reception	
Basement 1	Bellefonte Room	

Listen to a short conversation, and choose the best answer to each question.

6. What kind of event is the woman planning?

(A) An orientation
(B) A retirement celebration
(C) A product demonstration
(D) An examination

7. Look at the graphic. Which room does the Henderson Event Space say is available?

(A) The McPherson Room
(B) The Kinsen Room
(C) The Weldon Room
(D) The Bellefonte Room

8. What do the speakers agree to do?

(A) Reschedule a workshop
(B) Contact a supervisor
(C) Call Henderson Event Space
(D) Print some manuals

Listen to a short talk, and choose the best answer to each question.

9. According to the speaker, what will begin on Monday?

(A) A yearly sale
(B) A local festival
(C) A job fair
(D) A trade show

10. What does the speaker ask listeners to do?

(A) Assign work to a department member
(B) Attend a training session
(C) Update some computer software
(D) Mark a date on their calendar

11. Who is Jade Rivers?

(A) A city official
(B) A store manager
(C) A computer expert
(D) An event organizer

☑ TIPS-9

キーワードは耳印！
⇒設問キーワード
　(Monday)の直後に
　ヒント

☑ TIPS-10

I'd like～をキャッチ！
⇒ask問題では、I'd like
　やI wantがヒント

☐ assign
　～を割り当てる
☐ training session
　修会

☑ TIPS-11

選択肢をタテ読み！
⇒Who問題。選択肢を見
　て、職業をつかむ

Choose the best answer to complete the sentence.

12. The factory had to be closed down for a couple of days ------- a fault in one of the machines.

(A) due to
(B) because
(C) since
(D) as with

13. Software updates which resolve many of the issues raised by users will be released -------.

(A) shorten
(B) shortly
(C) shortness
(D) short

14. It is important that the training seminar start ------- delay as the room has been booked by another division immediately afterward.

(A) until
(B) unless
(C) except
(D) without

15. -------, Ridgemont Farms is the strongest it has ever been despite the unfavorable weather.

(A) Financial
(B) Financially
(C) Finance
(D) Financer

16. The design of the new Gregor Bank building is unremarkable ------- the huge doors at the main entrance.

(A) ever since
(B) according to
(C) apart from
(D) instead of

Choose the best answer to complete the text.
Questions 17-20 refer to the following advertisement.

The Tullox backpack --------- 17. with the busy lifestyles of today's young people in mind. It has a revolutionary design and modern features that active urban professionals will appreciate. --------- 18., it has a price tag that puts it within the grasp of almost anyone.

The material contains revolutionary fibers that repel water and dirt, keeping your bag looking new and its contents clean and dry. It also features a battery pack which can be used to charge a smartphone or even power a laptop computer. --------- 19.. They are on sale now --------- 20. quality clothing and accessories are sold.

□ revolutionary
革命的な
□ feature 特徴
□ appreciate ～ を
く評価する
□ price tag 価格タグ
□ repel ～をはじく

17. (A) will be designed
(B) has designed
(C) designs
(D) is designed

18. (A) Furthermore
(B) Therefore
(C) Despite
(D) Accordingly

19. (A) We are looking for investors to help launch this exciting product.
(B) The traditional appearance appeals to people with an eye for classic design.
(C) Manufactured in the Tullox factories in the UK, quality is assured.
(D) It is available only from the Tullox online store.

20. (A) as long as
(B) wherever
(C) whatever
(D) insomuch as

Choose the best answer for each question.
Questions 21-24 refer to the following online chat discussion.

Clinton Door [11:30 A.M.]:
We'll be arriving at the rest area in about 10 minutes. What time do you want to tell the passengers to be back on the bus?

Helga Rutter [11:31 A.M.]:
Let's say 12:00. It's easy for everyone to remember.

Martin Lawson [11:31 A.M.]:
Will we make it to the restaurant by 12:40? How about 11:50?

Donna Pau [11:32 A.M.]:
My bus is well behind you guys. We got caught in traffic after we left the museum. I don't think my passengers would have enough time to use the bathroom. I like Helga's suggestion better.

Clinton Door [11:33 A.M.]:
The lunch reservation isn't too important. We're the only group using the venue so they won't mind if we're a few minutes late.

Martin Lawson [11:35 A.M.]:
Fair enough.

Helga Rutter [11:37 A.M.]:
Should we call and let the hotel know what time we'll be arriving?

Clinton Door [11:45 A.M.]:
It might be worthwhile. I think we'll be arriving a little ahead of schedule. They might be able to get the rooms ready earlier.

Donna Pau [11:46 A.M.]:
I'll call them now. I'll tell them we'll be there just before 2:00 P.M.

Clinton Door [11:49 A.M.]:
Great. Thanks, Donna.

□ get caught in traffic
渋滞にあう
□ ahead of schedule
予定より早く

21. Who most likely are the writers?

(A) Tour guides
(B) Store clerks
(C) Truck drivers
(D) Travel agents

22. What was Ms. Pau delayed?

(A) There were some mechanical difficulties.
(B) She had to finish some work.
(C) The roads were congested.
(D) She lost her way.

23. What time will they leave the rest area?

(A) At 11:50 A.M.
(B) At 12:00 NOON
(C) At 12:10 P.M.
(D) At 12:40 P.M.

24. At 11:45 P.M., what does Mr. Door mean when he says, "It might be worthwhile"?

(A) He thinks that the restaurant is likely to be popular.
(B) He thinks they should warn the hotel that they will be early.
(C) He thinks they should spend longer at the rest stop.
(D) He thinks that the vehicles should be serviced more regularly.

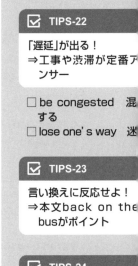

☑ **TIPS-22**

「遅延」が出る！
⇒工事や渋滞が定番ア
　ンサー

☐ be congested　混
　する
☐ lose one's way　迷

☑ **TIPS-23**

言い換えに反応せよ！
⇒本文back on the
　busがポイント

☑ **TIPS-24**

前後の文脈を読む！
⇒セオリー通り、ター
　ゲット文の前後の意
　味を取る

☐ warn　通告する
☐ rest stop　休憩所
☐ be serviced　保守
　検する

【ダブル＆トリプル・パッセージ問題】（Part7）〈広告＆メール〉のように、複数の文章を読んで解く問題です。文章量が多いので、設問の先読みは必須。効率的に読むことが重要です。

part1 46

Look at the picture and choose the statement that best describes what you see.

1. (A) (B) (C) (D)

☑ TIPS-1

「自転車の立てかけ」
が出る！

☐ grasp ～をつかむ
☐ reach for ～に手を
伸ばす
☐ be paved 舗装され
ている
☐ be propped up
against ～に立てか
けられている

2.(A) (B) (C) (D)

☑ TIPS-2

目立つものを見る！
⇒机の位置や書類、低い
仕切り、植物など

☐ plant 鉢植え
☐ be suspended 吊り
下げられている
☐ artwork 絵画
☐ partition 仕切り

Choose the best response to each question or statement.

3. (A) (B) (C)

4. (A) (B) (C)

5. (A) (B) (C)

Tuesday, March 23	Meet with Doug Walsh from Radio BTF.
Wednesday, March 24	Research and Development Meeting (In Boston)
Thursday, March 25	Attend Conference in Las Vegas
Friday, March 26	Day Off (Attend Smith wedding)

Listen to a short conversation, and choose the best answer to each question.

6. Who most likely are the speakers?

(A) Advertising executives
(B) Product reviewers
(C) Fashion experts
(D) Factory floor managers

7. Look at the graphic. When will the speakers most likely meet?
(A) On Tuesday
(B) On Wednesday
(C) On Thursday
(D) On Friday

8. Why does the man say he will invite Mr. Smith?
(A) To offer advice on customer service
(B) To discuss a production goal
(C) To help calculate some costs
(D) To learn about his employment history

☑ **TIPS**

「頻度」は頻出！
⇒「How often→数字」の
　パターンを攻略しよう

☑ **TIPS-6**

会社の役職に注意！
⇒Who問題。役職・職域
　も出題の定番

□ executive　重役
□ reviewer　批評家

☑ **TIPS-7**

クロス問題を攻略！
⇒会話と図表を対応さ
　せる

☑ **TIPS-8**

Mr.Smithの後を聞け！
⇒キーワード
　(Mr.Smith)の後、help
　をキャッチしよう

□ production goal
　生産目標
□ employment histor
　職歴

Listen to a short talk, and choose the best answer to each question.

9. Why is the speaker calling the customer?

(A) To announce a price reduction
(B) To discuss a problem with a project
(C) To offer a new service
(D) To introduce a new employee

10. Why does the speaker apologize?

(A) Some products arrived late.
(B) He was not available for a meeting.
(C) A deadline will not be met.
(D) He misunderstood a request.

11. What has the speaker sent to the customer?

(A) Some contact information
(B) Some parts for a device
(C) An updated schedule
(D) A letter from an inspector

☑ **TIPS-9**

I'm callingの後が
「要件」！
⇒電話問題の定番。冒頭
　に集中しよう

☐ price reduction
　値下げ

☑ **TIPS-10**

「謝罪」の理由は？
⇒I'm sorry, butの後
　にヒント

☐ deadline　締め切り
☐ misunderstand
　～を誤解する

☑ **TIPS-11**

追加情報は終盤！
⇒選択肢の名詞を先読
　みして、終盤に集中

Choose the best answer to complete the sentence.

12. Many of the employees indicated that they would ------- take time off than attend a retreat during the summer.

(A) rather
(B) prefer
(C) well
(D) better

☑ TIPS-12

wouldがヒント。
⇒[would（　）A than B]

□ retreat　隠れ家

13. None of the applicants for the junior sales clerk position had any ------- experience.

(A) former
(B) prior
(C) much
(D) neither

☑ TIPS-13

履歴書の定番！
⇒[（　）experience]

□ applicant　応募者
□ sales clerk　定員

14. The segment of the M1 Highway between Freeman and Hillvale was made ------- to accommodate the extra traffic resulting from nearby housing developments.

(A) widest
(B) widen
(C) widely
(D) wider

☑ TIPS-14

make+O+C→
be made Cで考える！
⇒[make（　）]

□ segment　区切り
□ accommodate　〜を
　収容する

15. Sales of pool accessories are ------- in early summer when people start enjoying the outdoors more.

(A) highly
(B) highest
(C) height
(D) heighten

☑ TIPS-15

文法の盲点！
⇒theと（形容詞の）最上
　級の関係

16. The accounting department approved all but the ------- of Mr. Drysdale's purchase requests.

(A) expensive
(B) expensively
(C) most expensive
(D) expense

☑ TIPS-16

空所前のtheがポイント！

□ accounting
　department　経理部
□ approve　〜を承認す
　る
□ purchase request
　購入依頼

Choose the best answer to complete the text.
Questions 17-20 refer to the following article.

In Japan, when people travel, it is customary to bring a gift for those they meet at their destination and also for those waiting for them when they return. ‑‑‑‑‑‑‑‑ , omiyage or gift giving, is a huge business in Japan.
17.
Airports and train stations have rows and rows of stores offering a wide variety of local ‑‑‑‑‑‑‑‑ for travelers to take home with them. When
18.
traveling in Japan on business or for pleasure, it is important to follow this wonderful tradition. ‑‑‑‑‑‑‑‑. But it can also serve as an ice-breaker and
19.
a token of goodwill that may go a long way toward ‑‑‑‑‑‑‑‑. a meaningful
20.
relationship.

□ customary
習慣的な
□ row 列
□ ice-breaker 緊張を
ほぐすもの
□ a token of
〜のしるしに
□ goodwill 善意
□ go a long way 十分
である

17. (A) Nevertheless
(B) Similarly
(C) At least
(D) Indeed

18. (A) delicacies
(B) tours
(C) pastimes
(D) views

19. (A) It is hardly something that you should try to do for yourself.
(B) On the other hand, it is rare to bring something back from a holiday.
(C) At the very least, it will demonstrate your respect for local culture.
(D) This ancient custom is no longer popular these days.

20. (A) desiring
(B) establishing
(C) concluding
(D) evaluating

☑ **TIPS-17**

「強調」の副詞は？
⇒「お土産は慣例」→
「お土産は巨大ビジネ
ス」の流れ

☑ **TIPS-18**

消去法を上手く使う！
⇒「お土産」でない選択
肢はカット

☑ **TIPS-19**

お土産に「プラス」の文脈！
⇒文選択問題。否定語を
含む選択肢はカット

□ hardly
ほとんど〜ない
□ rare まれである
□ no longer もはや〜
ない

☑ **TIPS-20**

フレーズを意識しよう！
⇒[( ) a relationship]

Choose the best answer for each question.

Questions 21-25 refer to the following e-mail and survey.

To:	Donna Sanders
From:	Bill Hanson
Date:	June 2
Subject:	Survey results
Attachment:	survey

Ms. Sanders,

As you know, we have installed touch screens in all of the tables at our stores across the United States. These screens are used to display our menus, take orders and to advertise promotional events and vacant positions in the restaurant. In recent months, we have been using the screen to conduct surveys of diners' experiences at the restaurant. People who take the time to fill out a survey get a discount of five percent on their meal.

You are probably already aware that the restaurant is getting ready for a major overhaul. In September this year, every Rockman's Diner in the country will have its interior updated. We are currently in negotiations with an interior designer that will carry out the work. We aim to have every location in the country refurbished within a month, so there is little we can do about that situation until then.

I've attached a survey that is representative of a lot of the feedback we have received. I would like to one of the issues mentioned in it when we meet. Thanks!

Bill Hanson
CEO Rockman's Diner

☐ advertise ～を宣伝する
☐ conduct surveys 調査する
☐ get a discount 割引してもらう
☐ overhaul 見直し
☐ refurbish 一新する

Rockman's Diner works hard to please its loyal clients and we hope to find ways in which our service can be improved and respond to our customer's needs.

Respondent: Hina Tani
Location: 600 N Clark St, Chicago, IL 60610

Why did you choose to dine at Rockman's Diner? It has a friendly atmosphere. My children like the children's menu.

Please comment on the following:

The dining room
The furniture and the interior design are getting a bit old. It is comfortable enough, but not very modern. The lighting in the booth we sat in was a bit too bright.

Food
The food was fine. We often eat here so we know what to expect. However, it would be nice to have some new items on the menu. I am getting a little tired of eating the same thing.

Service
Service is fast and friendly. Now that we have the touch screens, we don't have much of an opportunity to speak with the staff.

Thank you for your time. Please visit us again.

□ lighting　照明
□ Now that ～
　今や～なので

21. Who most likely is Ms. Sanders?

(A) A restaurant manager
(B) A food critic
(C) An advertising executive
(D) A technology expert

☑ TIPS-21

Ms.Sandersが目印！
⇒Who問題。パッセージ
1の冒頭にヒント

22. What is NOT a function of the restaurant's touchscreens?

(A) Taking meal orders
(B) Providing entertainment
(C) Showing menu offerings
(D) Advertising employment opportunities

☑ TIPS-22

キーワード周辺を読む！
⇒NOT問題。
　Touchscreensを
　サーチして、選択肢と
　比較

□ take orders
　注文する
□ employment
　opportunity　雇用機会

23. What is implied about Ms. Tani?

(A) She visited Rockman's on business.
(B) She rarely eats at Rockman's.
(C) She received a discount on her meal.
(D) She was interviewed by Ms. Sanders.

☑ TIPS-23

imply問題は要注意！
⇒クロス問題だが、
　パッセージ2だけでも
　回答可

□ on business　商用で

24. In the survey, the word, "ways" in paragraph 1 is closest in meaning to

(A) methods
(B) aspects
(C) directions
(D) functions

☑ TIPS-24

語彙は文脈を見る！
⇒すぐに選択肢を選ん
　ではダメ

25. What is likely to be discussed at the meeting?

(A) Furnishings
(B) Menu variety
(C) Customer service
(D) Cleanliness

 TIPS-25

これから何が議論される?
⇒survey(パッセージ2)
　の示す問題点にヒント

【ダブル＆トリプル・パッセージ問題】（Part7）　最大の難所は、二つ（三つ）
の文章を読み、情報を関連させて解く「クロス問題」です。「人名」「日付」「製品名」
がクロス問題の目印！

part 1 50

Look at the picture and choose the statement that best describes what
you see.

1. (A) (B) (C) (D)

2. (A) (B) (C) (D)

TIPS-1

人のいない写真が出る！
⇒そこでは、「人」関連の
　語句（passengers
　等）はバツ

☐ file
　列になって乗り込む
☐ vacant　空席の
☐ conductor　車掌

TIPS-2

Dinersが出る！
⇒レストランで席が埋
　まっている写真は定番

☐ be stacked
　積み上げられている
☐ fold away
　折りたたむ
☐ diner　食事する人
☐ sidewalk　歩道

Choose the best response to each question or statement.

3. (A) (B) (C)

4. (A) (B) (C)

5. (A) (B) (C)

part**3** 52

Listen to a short conversation, and choose the best answer to each question.

6. Where will the restaurant be located?

(A) At the seashore
(B) In the city center
(C) Next to a train station
(D) Beside a park

7. Who most likely is Rebecca Todd?

(A) A travel agent
(B) A city official
(C) A chef
(D) A construction worker

8. What does the woman say she will do?

(A) Contact a client
(B) Attend a seminar
(C) Visit a building site
(D) Read some instructions

Listen to a short talk, and choose the best answer to each question.

9. Who most likely is taking part in the tour?

(A) Nutritionists
(B) Supermarket owners
(C) Factory floor managers
(D) Sales representatives

10. Where will the tour begin?

(A) In the laboratory
(B) In the bakery
(C) In the shipping department
(D) In the sales office

11. What will participants be given at the end of the tour?

(A) Discount vouchers
(B) A uniform
(C) Product samples
(D) A product catalog

☑ **TIPS-9**

ツアー(job training)の対象は？
⇒Who問題。ツアーの目的・対象は冒頭

☑ **TIPS-10**

We'll startが耳印！

☐ laboratory　実験室

☑ **TIPS-11**

選択肢のタテ読み！
⇒選択肢を先読みして、ツアー最後のプレゼントを予測

Choose the best answer to complete the sentence.

12. The Montgomery Museum has announced ------- plans that will provide it with an additional 200 square meters of exhibition space.

(A) consideration
(B) expansion
(C) designation
(D) formation

13. Many visitors to the Vandelay Hotel are surprised at how ------- the lobby is.

(A) probable
(B) additional
(C) luxurious
(D) resourceful

14. The company has found it hard to ------- the success it had with its first range of products.

(A) afford
(B) reverse
(C) attend
(D) repeat

15. Megaform's new software allows businesses to ------- predict consumer demand based on a wide range of factors.

(A) accurately
(B) respectfully
(C) ignorantly
(D) subtly

16. The HYH Building in central Chicago was ------- by the renowned architect, Max Walsh.

(A) concerned
(B) designed
(C) distributed
(D) enlisted

✓ TIPS12-15

コロケーションから解く！
⇒選択肢の品詞が同じ→
語彙問題。意味からで
はなく、空所前後の単
語との「慣用」や「相性」
で決める。知らないと
解けないのも特徴

☐ additional　追加の
☐ exhibition space
示スペース

☐ predict
～を予見する
☐ consumer demand
消費者要請
☐ a wide range of
広範囲の

✓ TIPS-16

受け身をほどく！
⇒[The building was
（　）]→[（　）the
building]と考える

☐ renowned　有名な
☐ architect　建築科

Choose the best answer to complete the text.
Questions 17-20 refer to the following e-mail.

To:	All Employees
From:	Roseanne Wiley
Date:	October 2
Subject:	Employee leave

Dear All,

It seems that some-------- is needed regarding the company's policy
17.
for paid days off. Each employee is entitled to 20 personal days off per
year.

-------- In addition to personal days, employees may take up to five
18.
days off for -------- purposes. It is necessary to bring a doctor's
19.
certificate when taking such days. In addition to these types of leave,
we also allow employees to take up to four days a year to attend to
family matters. You may discuss the specifics of this type of leave with
your immediate supervisor. Please remember that people still in their
first 12 months of employment are only -------- the standard allotment
20.
of personal days.

Sincerely,
Roseanne May
General Manager

☐ days off　休暇
☐ be entitled to
　～する資格がある
☐ certificate　証明書
☐ leave　休暇
☐ immediate supervisor
　直属の上司
☐ allotment　割当、分配

☑ TIPS-17

パート6の語彙は文脈！
⇒意味からだと解けない

☑ TIPS-18

プラス文脈から解く！
⇒「休暇取得」の文脈な
　ので、否定語を含む選
　択肢はカット

☐ from now on
　今から
☐ be eligible for
　～に適任である
☐ register
　～を登録する

☑ TIPS-19

空所後のdoctorが
ヒント！

17. (A) tradition
    (B) attempt
    (C) recommendation
    (D) clarification

18. (A) These may be taken at any time for any reason at all.
    (B) From now on, no other kind of leave is being offered.
    (C) You will not be eligible for these for your first three years.
    (D) As a city employee, you must register a month in advance.

19. (A) volunteering
    (B) educational
    (C) medical
    (D) financial

20. (A) compiled
　　(B) entitled
　　(C) disturbed
　　(D) satisfied

☑ TIPS-20

選選択肢の品詞が同じ！
⇒語彙問題。[People
　are 〜ed]のカタチが
　ヒント

part 7

Choose the best answer for each question.

Questions 21-25 refer to the following brochure, e-mail, and policy statement.

Newhart Office Furniture

Newhart Office Furniture strives to offer its customers the best possible value for money by stocking only goods with the highest cost-performance ratio. While our range is limited by most stores' standards, you can feel assured that no matter which of our products you choose, you are getting a quality item.

Visit one of our showrooms in New York, Chicago, Los Angeles, Huston or Miami. Otherwise, you can shop online at our Web site, www. newhartof. com.

Office Chairs

Remway C90 12-month warranty $245.00 each	CoolBro 2020 5-year warranty $230.00 each
Softimax SFC 2-year warranty $190.00 each	Reclinoking FB2 3-year warranty $170.00 each

This month, there is a 25 percent discount on all online orders. Act now as online stock is limited. Our regional stores are offering 10 percent discounts for purchases totaling $2,000 or more. Contact your local store for further details.

☐ strive　努力する
☐ regional　地方の

To:	Glenda Rose <grose@sloughfinance.com>
From:	Bob Vance <bvance@sloughfinance.com>
Date:	March 23
Subject:	New office chairs

Dear Glenda,

I have taken a look at the brochure for new office chairs that you sent. I think we should consider expenses like this in the long-term so I would you like to get the model with the best warranty. They are all reasonably priced so that does not seem like a big issue.

I noticed that there is a significant discount for online orders this month. Let's take advantage of that.

After you have placed the order, send the invoice to Brad Collins in accounting. He will ensure payment is carried out by the end of the day.

Thanks,

Bob Vance
General Manager — Slough Finance

☐ brochure
パンフレット
☐ warranty 保証
☐ place the order 注文する
☐ invoice 請求書、送り状
☐ ensure ～を確実にする

Thank you for purchasing a quality item from Newhart Office Furniture.

All products we sell are covered by manufacturers' warranties. Nevertheless, should there be any problems with the quality of the items, Newhart Office Furniture will accept full responsibility and provide replacements or repairs on behalf of the manufacturers. Faulty items purchased at our regional stores will be collected by a store representative. Items purchased online, however, should be returned to our warehouse in Seattle, Washington. You may do this by sending the item using Amertrans Delivery Service.

☐ responsibility 責任
☐ replacement 交換
☐ on behalf of ～に代わって
☐ faulty items 欠陥品
☐ representative 担当者
☐ warehouse 倉庫

21. In the brochure, the word "while" in paragraph 1, line 3 is closest in meaning to

(A) As long as
(B) During the time
(C) Even though
(D) Whereas

☑ TIPS-21

語彙は文脈を見る！
⇒[While A, B]

22. What is indicated about Newhart Office Furniture?

(A) It has stores in multiple cities.
(B) It stocks a wide variety of brands.
(C) It manufactures its own product line.
(D) It sells goods exclusively online.

23. Which chair will Ms. Rose most likely choose?

(A) Remway C90
(B) CoolBro 2020
(C) Softimax SFC
(D) Reclinoking FB2

24. How can customers at regional stores obtain a price reduction?

(A) By purchasing designated sale items
(B) By spending over a certain amount
(C) By using a voucher included with the brochure
(D) By registering as a corporate customer

25. What is implied about Ms. Rose's order?

(A) A company representative will visit her if there is a problem.
(B) It will be delivered after new stock has been ordered.
(C) It does not qualify for any kind of discount.
(D) She should send any defective items to Seattle.

✓ TIPS-22

会社の特徴を探せ！
⇒選択肢の名詞を軸に
　パッセージ1と比較

☐ multiple　複数の
☐ a wide variety of
　幅広い
☐ manufacture
　〜を製造する
☐ exclusively　独占的

✓ TIPS-23

クロス問題を攻略！
⇒ パッセージ2で
　Ms.Rose、次にパッセ
　ージ1の図表をサーチ

✓ TIPS-24

「割引」はパンフの終盤！
⇒パッセージ1の終盤
　discountsをサーチ

☐ designated
　指定された
☐ voucher　クーポン
☐ corporate　法人の

✓ TIPS-25

パッセージ3の役割を見
抜く！
⇒「保証」の文章からポイ
　ントを推測

☐ qualify
　〜の資格を与える
☐ defective items　欠
　品

CHAPTER

14

【ダブル＆トリプル・パッセージ問題】(Part7)　SI と NOT は難問のサインです。設問に suggest, indicate, imply, NOT を含む場合、本文と選択肢の比較検討が必須！

part1　🎧 54

Look at the picture and choose the statement that best describes what you see.

1. (A) (B) (C) (D)

✓ TIPS-1

意外な単語に注意！
⇒addressを動詞で使うと？

☐ face　～に向く
☐ address　～に話しかける

2.(A) (B) (C) (D)

✓ TIPS-2

リスニングの精度を上げよう！
⇒動詞キャッチの「次」を目指す

☐ grasp
　～をしっかりと握る
☐ position　～を置く

part2 55

Choose the best response to each question or statement.

3. (A) (B) (C)

4. (A) (B) (C)

5. (A) (B) (C)

☑ **TIPS**

Don't you~?
= Do you~?
⇒「否定疑問文」を「普通
の疑問文」と捉える

☐ come along　うま〈
進む

part3 56

Listen to a short conversation, and choose the best answer to each question.

6. What is the conversation mainly about?

(A) A new health club
(B) A company banquet
(C) A cycling group
(D) A shopping trip

☑ **TIPS-6**

最初のセリフに集中！
⇒会話の目的を問う問
題なので、セオリー通
りに

☐ banquet　宴会

7. What does the man say will happen tomorrow?
(A) Event details will be published.
(B) Membership fees will be collected.
(C) People will vote on a decision.
(D) Some new equipment will arrive.

☑ **TIPS-7**

男性のセリフを聞く！
⇒設問の主語＝男性。
男性のセリフにヒント

☐ publish
　　～を公表する
☐ vote　～に投票する

8. What does the man plan to bring?

(A) A set of luggage
(B) An instruction manual
(C) A map of the area
(D) A list of accommodations

☑ **TIPS-8**

「これから」はI'llを
待ち伏せ！
⇒男性のセリフで、男性
のアクションを聞こう

☐ luggage　カバン
☐ accommodation　
　宿泊施設

Listen to a short talk, and choose the best answer to each question.

9. What is the announcement mainly about?
(A) A new rail service
(B) A discount ticket offer
(C) A station policy update
(D) A change of boarding location

✓ TIPS-9

「お詫び」の次を聞く！
⇒不具合のお詫び→
　代替案という流れ

10. According to the announcement, what should listeners do?
(A) Use a smartphone application
(B) Check a display
(C) Ask for a refund
(D) Fill out a form

✓ TIPS-10

Please～?が耳印！
⇒「お願い文」
　Would you～?や
　Please～?にヒント

☐ refund　返金
☐ fill out　～に記入する

11. When will the next train for Richmond leave?
(A) In 5 minutes
(B) In 10 minutes
(C) In 15 minutes
(D) In 20 minutes

✓ TIPS-11

Richmondを耳印にし
て、「時」をキャッチ！

Choose the best answer to complete the sentence.

12. HRT Engineering was praised for the ------- of its solution to the problems faced by bridge builders.

(A) simplicity
(B) prematurity
(C) resemblance
(D) attribution

13. The design department employees have asked for an opportunity to ------- with the staff in market research.

(A) exceed
(B) converse
(C) ascertain
(D) persuade

14. Viewers of Channel 10's popular new documentary series were ------- to learn that it had been canceled.

(A) competed
(B) desired
(C) favored
(D) disappointed

15. Maintenance of Gordon Park on Neil Street is paid for by a local historical ------- society.

(A) destination
(B) preservation
(C) competition
(D) presentation

16. A list of ------- sites for the company's new office is being considered by upper management.

(A) immediate
(B) promotional
(C) potential
(D) responsible

TIPS-12

カタマリを変換してみる！
⇒[the (N) of its
　solution]→
　[the (形) solution]

□ praise　〜を称賛する

TIPS-13

自動詞を探せ！
⇒[(　) with 人]

□ opportunity　機会
□ market research
　市場調査

TIPS-14

語法から解く！
⇒[be (　) to do]

□ viewer　視聴者

TIPS-15

形容詞との相性を見る！
⇒[a local historical
　(　) society]

□ maintenance　整備
□ be paid for
　支払われる

TIPS-16

コロケーションを意識
しよう！
⇒[(　) site]

100

Choose the best answer to complete the text.
Questions 17-20 refer to the following advertisement.

Ragamuffin brand watches are made for people who are looking for something a little out of the ---------- 17. They are ---------- 18. crafted and come with a five-year warranty on parts and labor. Their designs identify the ---------- 19. as a fun-loving individual who is not afraid to be different. They are available only at highly respected watch sellers and department stores that stock the top brands. ---------- 20. To learn more about this option, speak with store staff or visit our Web site at www.ragamuffin.com Wear a Ragamuffin watch and stand out from the crowd!

☐ craft
　～を念入りに作る
☐ come with
　～を備えた
☐ warranty　保証
☐ identify A as B　AをBとみなす、証明する
☐ fun-loving　楽しむことが好きな
☐ stand out　目立つ

17. (A) question
(B) budget
(C) promotion
(D) ordinary

TIPS-17

広告はプラスの文脈！
⇒消費を促す表現をイメージする

18. (A) expertly
(B) expert
(C) expertise
(D) experts

TIPS-18

選択肢の品詞がバラバラ!
⇒品詞問題。空所は副詞

19. (A) driver
(B) reader
(C) wearer
(D) performer

TIPS-19

「腕時計」をする人は？

20. (A) As a matter of policy, Ragamuffin watches never go on sale.
(B) We have payment plans for customers purchasing items priced at $600 or more.
(C) You can buy a Ragamuffin watches are only sold online.
(D) Call now to have your watch serviced by our trained technicians.

TIPS-20

「入手方法」の文脈！
⇒文選択問題。
　入手方法・支払い・問い合わせの流れ

☐ go on sale　発売する
☐ payment　支払い

Choose the best answer for each question.

Questions 21-25 refer to the following Web page, letter to the editor, and article.

---

www.cantoncity.org/programs/cfiip

The Canton City Official Web Site

Programs
The CFIP (The Canton Filmmakers' Incentive Program)

Under the leadership of the Canton City Mayor, the city council has approved a plan to attract filmmakers to the area. The plan makes it very easy for filmmakers to get approval to use public areas for film shoots and ensures maximum cooperation from the city. This includes help hiring actors for crowd scenes and supply of free mobile office space for cast and crews to use.

The ultimate goal of the plan is to sure up the local economy by attracting more tourists to the area. In coming years, we will see how this plays out. There is good reason to be optimistic. Similar plans have been successful in towns with less to attract production companies than this one.

Canton Gazette

To the editor:

Gina Forest's initiative is certainly attracting a lot of filmmakers to the area and mine is among many local businesses that have benefitted greatly from the plan. Not only do we receive meal orders from the cast and crew of the films, but we also have more customers who come from out of town to visit the locations used in their favorite films. Canton's population is growing rapidly and we are attracting more and more major businesses to the region, which has given us one of the best employment situations in the nation.

Nevertheless, I am writing to suggest that we put some restrictions on this program in future years. I feel that we now have too many film crews in town and they are competing with local residents for access to publicly owned land. This is starting to have a negative effect on the lifestyles of many locals.

Rhonda Lowes, Canton City

☐ incentive　報奨金
☐ approve　〜を承認する
☐ cooperation　協力
☐ local economy　地域経済
☐ optimistic　楽観的な

☐ initiative　主導権
☐ population　人口
☐ restriction　制限
☐ compete with
　〜と競う

Canton City Council Puts Residents First

(June 5)—The Canton City Council released a press release this week to announce that it would be limiting the number of films that can be shot here each year. At present, the town is hosting as many as 15 film crews a year.

The new regulation limits the number to one per month, with no more than two film crews in town at any one time.

21. What is NOT a form of assistance provided by CFIP?

(A) Providing permission to make films in publicly owned areas
(B) Lowering of taxation rates for production companies
(C) Assisting with finding people to take minor parts in films
(D) Arranging complimentary office space

22. Who most likely is Gina Forest?

(A) A mayor
(B) A local businessperson
(C) A financial expert
(D) A journalist

23. What kind of business does Ms. Lowes most likely run?

(A) A production company
(B) A garden center
(C) A restaurant
(D) A talent agency

24. What objective of the program does Ms. Lowes mention in her letter?

(A) Boosting the population
(B) Increasing tourism
(C) Providing employment
(D) Improving public amenities

25. What is indicated about the Canton City Council?

(A) It carried out a survey of local residents.
(B) It agreed with Ms. Lowes' suggestion.
(C) It is receiving less benefit from CFIP than it anticipated.
(D) It is planning to run a film festival.

TOEIC テストでは、「設問」力が重要です。何が問われていて、そのヒントはど
こにあるのかをいち早く見抜かないと、時間内に回答は不可能です。最後に、設
問を意識して、解いてみましょう。

part **1** 58

Look at the picture and choose the statement that best describes what
you see.

1. (A) (B) (C) (D)

2. (A) (B) (C) (D)

---

part2 🎧 59

Choose the best response to each question or statement.

3. (A) (B) (C)

4. (A) (B) (C)

5. (A) (B) (C)

☑ **TIPS**

音の反復は不正解！
⇒Qと同じ音がAで聞
こえたらバツ

☐ air conditioning unit
空調ユニット
☐ convention　会議

part3 🎧 60

Listen to a short conversation, and choose the best answer to each question.

6. Where most likely are the speakers?

(A) In a restaurant
(B) In an art gallery
(C) In a hardware store
(D) In an appliance store

☑ **TIPS-6**

シチュエーションを
イメージ！
⇒冒頭のワードから
「場所」を見抜く

☐ hardware store　金
物店

7. What does the man ask about?

(A) A repair process
(B) A new menu item
(C) A lost item
(D) A price

☑ **TIPS-7**

男性の質問は？
⇒男性のセリフを聞こう

8. What will the woman most likely do next?

(A) Write out an invoice
(B) Take out a manual
(C) Look for a model number
(D) Telephone a colleague

☑ **TIPS-8**

I'llを待ち伏せ！
⇒do next問題。終盤の
女性のセリフにヒント

☐ invoice　請求書
☐ colleague　同僚

Listen to a short talk, and choose the best answer to each question.

9. What are the listeners participating in?

(A) A business conference
(B) A research study
(C) A sporting event
(D) A cooking competition

10. What types of samples will the listeners be given?

(A) Desserts
(B) Cleaning products
(C) Utensils
(D) Clothing items

11. What must listeners do to be paid?

(A) Fill out a form
(B) Win a competition
(C) Submit a receipt
(D) Publish a recipe

✓ TIPS-9

何の大会？
⇒冒頭に集中しよう

✓ TIPS-10

商品は何？
⇒大会の詳細は中盤。
　ワードからイメージ

✓ TIPS-11

willを待ち伏せ！
⇒You'll be paidが目
　印

☐ competition　競争
☐ receipt　領収書
☐ recipe　レシピ

Choose the best answer to complete the sentence.

12. When they join the company, employees are asked to sign a ------- stating that they will not share any confidential information.

(A) declaration
(B) consideration
(C) approval
(D) establishment

13. Max Winfield is a ------- visitor at Dino's Grille in Upper Manhattan.

(A) regional
(B) frequent
(C) respective
(D) complimentary

14. Durant Motors worked ------- with its partners at Harmon Engineering to produce its new sports car.

(A) hardly
(B) severely
(C) relatively
(D) closely

15. Applicants for the sales manager position had to perform well on a number of tests to ------- an interview with the company president.

(A) determine
(B) gain
(C) ready
(D) adhere

16. At her farewell party, Ms. Lewis received ------- for her years of hard work for the company.

(A) development
(B) revision
(C) recognition
(D) patience

Choose the best answer to complete the text.
Questions 17-20 refer to the following e-mail.

To:	Rudy Walsh <rwalsh@perfectviewps.com>
From:	Ignatius Jones <ijones@stantonmanor.com>
Date:	27 March
Subject:	Parking problems

Dear Rudy,

I have been -------- to come over and talk with you about the parking
17.
situation. Let me begin by saying that we -------- having Perfect
18.
View Photo Studio as a neighbor. Many of your customers spend
time at Stanton Manor while they wait for their appointment. --------.
19.
Nevertheless, in recent months, many of your customers have been
using our parking lot because yours is full. If I had ample parking, I
would not mention the issue. -------- , a recent survey of my customers
20.
has shown that the lack of parking discourages them from coming
here. Perhaps you could make an arrangement with one of our other
neighbors for your clients to use their parking lots instead.

Sincerely,

Ignatius Jones
Manager — Stanton Manor

☐ ample　広い
☐ discourage　思いと
　まらせる
☐ make an
　arrangement
　手配する

17. (A) causing
(B) attending
(C) revealing
(D) meaning

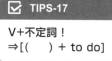

✓ TIPS-17

V+不定詞！
⇒[(　) + to do]

18. (A) enjoy
(B) resent
(C) oppose
(D) hesitate

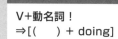

✓ TIPS-18

V+動名詞！
⇒[(　) + doing]

19. (A) We hope that you do not mind our use of your parking spaces.
   (B) I am glad we had this opportunity to speak directly.
   (C) Our lunchtime sales, in particular, are much-improved thanks to our location.
   (D) Let me know if you would like to shoot here again.

20. (A) Therefor
   (B) However
   (C) Otherwise
   (D) Whereas

☑ TIPS-19

直後のNevertheless
に注目！
⇒文選択問題。
Nevertheless前後
で、意味が逆転

☐ thanks to
　〜のおかげで
☐ shoot　〜を撮影する

☑ TIPS-20

空所前後の対比が重要！
⇒[A but B]を応用する

part 7

Choose the best answer for each question.
Questions 21-25 refer to the following online profile, e-mail, and survey form.

---

www.constantineanalytics.com/analystprofiles

Chuck Hwang

Chuck has a rare combination of experiences and expertise that makes him extremely valuable to companies looking to diversify their products and services or launch into new markets.

After graduating from Sterlington University with a master's degree in finance, he worked for five years at one of New York's best known financial institutions, during which time, he rose to the position of senior analyst.

He subsequently assumed a position at Devine Airlines. He led the team that launched Divine International, which enabled the company to provide international flights. Since then, he has taken several project management positions in major companies to oversee their expansion plans.

Contact our assignments officer at 23-55-3289 to discuss having Chuck assist with your project.

☐ combination　組み合わせ
☐ expertise　専門的技術、ノウハウ
☐ valuable　価値のある
☐ diversify　多様化する
☐ financial institution 金融機関
☐ subsequently　その後
☐ oversee 〜を監督する

To:	Gregory Cole <gcole@whippetbc.com>
From:	June Pompeo <jpompeo@constantineanalytics.com>
Subject:	Expansion plans
Date:	September 17

Dear Mr. Cole,

Thank you for contacting me about providing an analyst to help your team with their expansion into Canada. Whippet Bus Company is one of the largest and longest running bus companies in the United States and I would be proud to see you succeed across the border. For that reason, I am assigning you one of our most sought-after analysts, Chuck Huang.

He should already be very familiar with your brand as he grew up and went to university very near your corporate headquarters. I can assign him to your project for three months from September 20 to December 20. If you need someone to work longer than that, I can suggest another of our analysts. Her name is Freda Shimizu.

She is every bit as experienced and committed as Mr. Huang and the only reason that she is not my first choice is that she does not have the connection with Whippet Bus Company that Mr. Huang does.

□ expansion 拡大
□ assign ～を選任する

Constantine Analytics Evaluation Form

Evaluating officer: Gregory Cole **Company:** Whippet Bus Company
Position: Company president
Constantine Analyst: Freda Shimizu
Start date: September 20
Project type: Company expansion
Details: We opened our first office and bus service in Canada with Ms. Shimizu's assistance.
Overall satisfaction: Very high
Additional comments: I was amazed at how prepared Ms. Shimizu was. I had organized a meeting with our corporate executives to discuss our corporate history and company policies but found that Ms. Shimizu was already very knowledgeable and ready to start work immediately. I feel that the project could not have been nearly as successful without her assistance.

□ knowledgeable 知識
のある
□ immediately すぐに

21. In the online profile, the word "assumed" in paragraph 3, line 1 is closest in meaning to
(A) believed
(B) pretended
(C) undertook
(D) enhanced

☑ **TIPS-21**

文脈から推測！
⇒即答せずに、前後関係
　を見る

22. What is suggested about Mr. Huang?
(A) He has experience leading groups.
(B) He is a member of a professional association.
(C) He is on the Devine Airlines' board of directors.
(D) He will soon travel internationally on business.

☑ **TIPS-22**

suggest問題は要注意！
⇒パッセージ1と選択肢
　を比較検討

☐ association
　会社、提携
☐ board of directors
　取締役会

23. What is implied about Whippet Bus Company?

(A) It has an office in Canada.
(B) It is based in Sterlington.
(C) It is a new company.
(D) It has purchased some new vehicles.

☑ **TIPS-23**

クロス問題の応用！
⇒パッセージ1＆2。
　消去法で対応しよう

24. To whom did Ms. Pompeo send the e-mail?

(A) A business analyst
(B) A company president
(C) A bus driver
(D) An airline executive

☑ **TIPS-24**

クロス問題の定番！
⇒パッセージ１＆２。
　Ms.Pompeoをサー
　チすれば即答

25. What is implied about Whippet Bus Company's expansion?

(A) It took longer than three months.
(B) It went over budget.
(C) It received funding from the government.
(D) It was mentioned in the news.

☑ **TIPS-25**

imply問題も難問ぞろい！
⇒パッセージ2。選択肢
　との比較検討が必須

☐ budget　予算
☐ funding　資金

音声ファイルのダウンロード方法

英宝社ホームページ（http://www.eihosha.co.jp/）の
「テキスト音声ダウンロード」バナーをクリックすると、
音声ファイルダウンロードページにアクセスできます。

Fun and Strategies for TOEIC® Listening & Reading Test
TIPS で攻略する TOEIC® L&R テスト

2020 年 2 月 25 日　初　版	2024 年 3 月 25 日　第 3 刷

著　者ⓒ　塚　田　幸　光

発 行 者　佐 々 木　　元

発 行 所　株式会社　英　　宝　　社

〒101-0032 東京都千代田区岩本町 2-7-7
TEL 03 (5833) 5870-1　FAX 03 (5833) 5872

ISBN 978-4-269-66051-9 C3582
［製版・表紙デザイン：伊谷企画／印刷：日本ハイコム（株）］